Tcl/Tk 8.5 Programming Cookbook

Over 100 great recipes to effectively learn Tcl/Tk 8.5

Bert Wheeler

BIRMINGHAM - MUMBAI

Tcl/Tk 8.5 Programming Cookbook

First published: February 2011

Production Reference: 1080211

Published by Packt Publishing Ltd.
32 Lincoln Road
Olton
Birmingham, B27 6PA, UK.

ISBN 978-1-849512-98-5

www.packtpub.com

Cover Image by Asher Wishkerman (a.wishkerman@mpic.de)

Credits

Author
Bert Wheeler

Reviewers
Clif Flynt
Thomas J. Krehbiel

Acquisition Editor
Steven Wilding

Development Editor
Susmita Panda

Technical Editor
Pooja Pande

Indexer
Hemangini Bari

Editorial Team Leader
Aanchal Kumar

Project Team Leader
Ashwin Shetty

Project Coordinator
Joel Goveya

Proofreader
Jacqueline McGhee

Production Coordinator
Adline Swetha Jesuthas

Cover Work
Adline Swetha Jesuthas

About the Author

Bert Wheeler was born and raised in Louisville, Kentucky and is one of five sons. After graduating from high school he entered the United States Navy and later retired in 1997, after 20 years as an Air Traffic Controller. Following his military career, Bert returned to college and graduated Magna Cum Laude with a degree in computer science.

After completion of his degree, Bert worked in all aspects of the IT and software industries in numerous positions including Software Design and Development, Project and Product Management, Director of Information Technologies, and Director of Engineering Services. He continues to work and his primary area of expertise is in the design and implementation of physical security solutions in the Access Control arena throughout the world.

Acknowledgment

This book would not have been completed without the help of numerous individuals. I would like to thank the staff at Packt Publishing for their meticulous efforts and editorial assistance throughout the completion of this book. Special thanks to Steven Wilding, Susmita Panda, and Joel Goveya, whose tireless efforts have guided me and kept me on track.

As with all writers, it is our families that provide the support and necessary encouragement. To Claudia, my wife, partner and best friend, and my sons Jeremy, Justin, Valentino, and Arrigo. Without your love and support throughout my lifetime, I would not have become who I am today. Thank you for everything you have done, the lessons you have taught me and the love that keeps me going. I am blessed.

About the Reviewers

Clif Flynt has been a professional programmer since 1978. He has used languages ranging from Am2900 microcode to high level languages such as APL, HTML, and Tcl/Tk. Clif has developed applications for many clients including the US Navy, General Mills, and McDonalds, and also for his own amusement.

Clif has taught computer science at Grinnell College and Eastern Michigan University. He's a member of the Washtenaw Community College Computer Science Advisory Committee. He's delivered training sessions in the US, Canada, Europe, and India, and has given talks at conferences in the US and Europe.

Clif is the president and founder of the Tcl Community Association, the organization that runs the annual Tcl/Tk conference in the US and coordinates the Tcl/Tk and Open ACS involvement with Google Summer of Code. Since 1999, Clif has owned his own company: Noumena Corporation. Noumena Corporation provides computer training and software development services, focusing on Tcl/Tk and other open source technologies.

Clif has written *Tcl/Tk for Real Programmers*, *Tcl/Tk: A Developer's Guide*; has edited *Interactive Web Applications with Tcl/Tk* (Academic Press, Schroeder/Doyle), *Practical Programming in Tcl/Tk* (Prentice Hall, Welch/Jones/Hobbs), *Tcl and the Tk Toolkit* (Addison Wesley, Ousterhout/Jones), and *Tcl/Tk Programmer's Reference* (Osborne, Nelson).

Thomas J. Krehbiel is a graduate electrical engineer with a Masters' in solid state semiconductor and device physics. During his career in the semiconductor industry, he did IC circuit design, IC device design, managed a parametric test area, managed a CIM group, and worked in a RET (Reticle Enhancement Technologies) software development group. Along the way, he created a parametric data analysis system, a wafer tracking system, and a RET processing system.

Thomas has many years of experience managing software development and the hardware and system associated with that development. He has programmed for over 30 years, starting with FORTRAN and ending with his current favorite language Tcl/Tk. As computers changed, Tom worked with mainframes (IBM360), minis (DEC), and desktops (HPUX, Solaris, Linux, Windows).

When he was younger, he enjoyed playing baseball, basketball, handball, tennis, hiking the Grand Canyon, and snow skiing.

www.PacktPub.com

Support files, eBooks, discount offers and more

You might want to visit www.PacktPub.com for support files and downloads related to your book.

Did you know that Packt offers eBook versions of every book published, with PDF and ePub files available? You can upgrade to the eBook version at www.PacktPub.com and as a print book customer, you are entitled to a discount on the eBook copy. Get in touch with us at service@packtpub.com for more details.

At www.PacktPub.com, you can also read a collection of free technical articles, sign up for a range of free newsletters and receive exclusive discounts and offers on Packt books and eBooks.

http://PacktLib.PacktPub.com

Do you need instant solutions to your IT questions? PacktLib is Packt's online digital book library. Here, you can access, read and search across Packt's entire library of books.

Why Subscribe?

- Fully searchable across every book published by Packt
- Copy & paste, print and bookmark content
- On demand and accessible via web browser

Free Access for Packt account holders

If you have an account with Packt at www.PacktPub.com, you can use this to access PacktLib today and view nine entirely free books. Simply use your login credentials for immediate access.

Table of Contents

Preface

Created in 1988 by John Ousterhoult, while working at the University of Califormia, Berkeley, Tcl (Tool Command Language) is a scripting language originally designed for embedded system platforms. Since its creation, Tcl has grown far beyond its original design with numerous expansions and additions (such as the graphical Took Kit or Tk) to become a full-featured scripted programming language capable of creating elegant, cross-platform solutions.

This book is written for both the beginning developer looking for a instructions on how to get their application up and running quickly to the experienced Tcl/Tk programmer looking to sharpen their skills. You will find everything from utilization of the console commands through to the creation of a stand-alone application.

What this book covers

Chapter 1, The Tcl Shell, gives an introduction to the Tcl shell.

Chapter 2, Using the Building Blocks Control Constructs, talks about using control constructs (`if` statements, `for` statements, and so on) to perform control program flow.

Chapter 3, Error Handling, talks about using the built-in commands and the Tcl shell to perform error handling.

Chapter 4, Handling String Expressions, explains how to create, manipulate, and manage string variables.

Chapter 5, Expanding String Functionality Using List, shows how to create, manipulate, and manage data in Tcl lists.

Chapter 6, The Tcl Dictionary, explains how to create, manipulate, and manage data in Tcl dictionaries.

Chapter 7, File Operations, tells how to open, read, write, and configure access to files stored on the system.

Chapter 8, Tk GUI Programming with Tcl/Tk, gives an introduction to the Tk shell, creating and managing a widget or window.

Chapter 9, Configuring and Controlling Tk Widgets, explains about creating and managing the most commonly used Tk widgets.

Chapter 10, Geometry Management, talks about managing the layout and design of the window.

Chapter 11, Using Tcl Built-In Dialog Windows, is about the creation and use of the Tcl built-in dialog windows available in Tk.

Chapter 12, Creating and Managing Menus, explains creating and managing menus, menu buttons, and pop-up menus.

Chapter 13, Creating the Address Book Application, gives full code listing and description of an Address Book application that makes use of the information covered in the previous sections.

What you need for this book

To complete the recipes covered in this book you will need the following:

- A computer running any supported operating system (Window, Linux, Mac OSX, and so on)
- A standard installation of Tcl/Tk
  - Available at `www.tcl.tk`
- A non-formatting text editor such as Notepad

Who this book is for

If you are a beginner interested in adding Tcl/Tk 8.5 to your list of languages or an experienced Tcl/Tk programmer looking to sharpen your knowledge, be assured you will find your perfect guide in this book. Whether you are developing for your personal use or commercial applications, this book will provide you with a ready reference to the building blocks of Tcl/Tk 8.5.

Conventions

In this book, you will find a number of styles of text that distinguish between different kinds of information. Here are some examples of these styles, and an explanation of their meaning.

Code words in text are shown as follows: "The `catch` construct is used to prevent errors from aborting a script."

A block of code is set as follows:

```
If {[catch {set doubled [expr $value * 2]} errmsg]} {
puts "Script Failed - $errmsg"
} else {
puts "$value doubled is: $doubled"
}
```

Any command-line input or output is written as follows:

```
% unset x
%
```

New terms and **important words** are shown in bold. Words that you see on the screen, in menus or dialog boxes for example, appear in the text like this: "If the user clicks on the **Cancel** button, an empty string is returned."

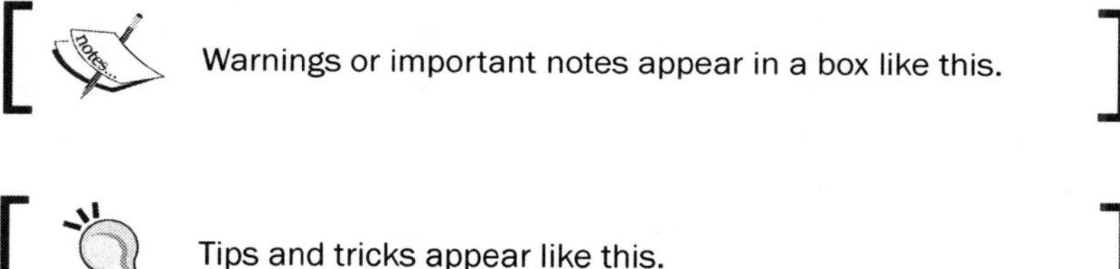

Warnings or important notes appear in a box like this.

Tips and tricks appear like this.

Reader feedback

Feedback from our readers is always welcome. Let us know what you think about this book—what you liked or may have disliked. Reader feedback is important for us to develop titles that you really get the most out of.

To send us general feedback, simply send an e-mail to `feedback@packtpub.com`, and mention the book title via the subject of your message.

If there is a book that you need and would like to see us publish, please send us a note in the **SUGGEST A TITLE** form on `www.packtpub.com` or e-mail `suggest@packtpub.com`.

If there is a topic that you have expertise in and you are interested in either writing or contributing to a book, see our author guide on `www.packtpub.com/authors`.

Customer support

Now that you are the proud owner of a Packt book, we have a number of things to help you to get the most from your purchase.

Downloading the example code for this book

You can download the example code files for all Packt books you have purchased from your account at `http://www.PacktPub.com`. If you purchased this book elsewhere, you can visit `http://www.PacktPub.com/support` and register to have the files e-mailed directly to you.

Errata

Although we have taken every care to ensure the accuracy of our content, mistakes do happen. If you find a mistake in one of our books—maybe a mistake in the text or the code—we would be grateful if you would report this to us. By doing so, you can save other readers from frustration and help us improve subsequent versions of this book. If you find any errata, please report them by visiting `http://www.packtpub.com/support`, selecting your book, clicking on the **errata submission form** link, and entering the details of your errata. Once your errata are verified, your submission will be accepted and the errata will be uploaded on our website, or added to any list of existing errata, under the Errata section of that title. Any existing errata can be viewed by selecting your title from `http://www.packtpub.com/support`.

Piracy

Piracy of copyright material on the Internet is an ongoing problem across all media. At Packt, we take the protection of our copyright and licenses very seriously. If you come across any illegal copies of our works, in any form, on the Internet, please provide us with the location address or website name immediately so that we can pursue a remedy.

Please contact us at `copyright@packtpub.com` with a link to the suspected pirated material.

We appreciate your help in protecting our authors, and our ability to bring you valuable content.

Questions

You can contact us at `questions@packtpub.com` if you are having a problem with any aspect of the book, and we will do our best to address it.

1
The Tcl Shell

In this chapter, we will cover the following topics:

- The Tcl shell
- Writing to the Tcl console
- Mathematical expressions
- Tcl `expr` operands
- Tcl `expr` operators
- Mathematical functions
- Computing mathematical expressions
- Referencing files in Tcl
- Variables
- Launching a Tcl script

Introduction

So, you've installed Tcl, written some scripts, and now you're ready to get a deeper understanding of Tcl and all that it has to offer. So, why are we starting with the shell when it is the most basic tool in the Tcl toolbox?

When I started using Tcl I needed to rapidly deliver a **Graphical User Interface** (**GUI**) to display a video from the IP-based network cameras. The solution had to run on Windows and Linux and it could not be browser-based due to the end user's security concerns. The client needed it quickly and our sales team had, as usual, committed to a delivery date without speaking to the developer in advance. So, with the requirement document in hand, I researched the open source tools available at the time and Tcl/Tk was the only language that met the challenge.

The original solution quickly evolved into a full-featured IP Video Security system with the ability to record and display historic video as well as providing the ability to attach to live video feeds from the cameras. Next search capabilities were added to review the stored video and a method to navigate to specific dates and times. The final version included configuring advanced recording settings such as resolution, color levels, frame rate, and variable speed playback. All was accomplished with Tcl.

Due to the time constraints, I was not able get a full appreciation of the capabilities of the shell. I saw it as a basic tool to interact with the interpreter to run commands and access the file system. When I had the time, I returned to the shell and realized just how valuable a tool it is and the many capabilities I had failed to make use of.

When used to its fullest, the shell provides much more that an interface to the Tcl interpreter, especially in the early stages of the development process. Need to isolate and test a procedure in a program? Need a quick debugging tool? Need real-time notification of the values stored in a variable? The Tcl shell is the place to go.

Since then, I have learned countless uses for the shell that would not only have sped up the development process, but also saved me several headaches in debugging the GUI and video collection. I relied on numerous dialog boxes to pop up values or turned to writing debugging information to error logs. While this was an excellent way to get what I needed, I could have minimized the overhead in terms of coding by simply relying on the shell to display the desired information in the early stages.

While dialog windows and error logs are irreplaceable, I now add in quick debugging by using the commands the shell has to offer. If something isn't proceeding as expected, I drop in a command to write to standard out and voila! I have my answer. The shell continues to provide me with a reliable method to isolate issues with a minimum investment of time.

The Tcl shell

The **Tcl Shell** (**Tclsh**) provides an interface to the Tcl interpreter that accepts commands from both standard input and text files. Much like the Windows Command Line or Linux Terminal, the Tcl shell allows a developer to rapidly invoke a command and observe the return value or error messages in standard output. The shell differs based on the Operating System in use. For the Unix/Linux systems, this is the standard terminal console; while on a Windows system, the shell is launched separately via an executable.

If invoked with no arguments, the shell interface runs interactively, accepting commands from the native command line. The input line is demarked with a percent sign (%) with the prompt located at the start position. If the shell is invoked from the command line (Windows DOS or Unix/Linux terminal) and arguments are passed, the interpreter will accept the first as the filename to be read. Any additional arguments are processed as variables. The shell will run until the `exit` command is invoked or until it has reached the end of the text file.

When invoked with arguments, the shell sets several Tcl variables that may be accessed within your program, much like the C family of languages. These variables are:

Variable	Explanation
`argc`	This variable contains the number of arguments passed in with the exception of the script file name. A value of 0 is returned if no arguments were passed in.
`argv`	This variable contains a Tcl List with elements detailing the arguments passed in. An empty string is returned if no arguments were provided.
`argv0`	This variable contains the filename (if specified) or the name used to invoke the Tcl shell.
`TCL_interactive`	This variable contains a '1' if Tclsh is running in interactive mode, otherwise a '0' is contained.
`env`	The `env` variable is maintained automatically, as an array in Tcl and is created at startup to hold the environment variables on your system.

Writing to the Tcl console

The following recipe illustrates a basic command invocation. In this example, we will use the `puts` command to output a "Hello World" message to the console.

Getting ready

To complete the following example, launch your Tcl Shell as appropriate, based on your operating platform. For example, on Windows, you would launch the executable contained in the Tcl installation location within the `bin` directory, while on a Unix/Linux installation, you would enter `TCLsh` at the command line, provided this is the executable name for your particular system. To check the name, locate the executable in the `bin` directory of your installation.

How to do it...

Enter the following command:

```
% puts "Hello World"
Hello World
```

How it works...

As you can see, the `puts` command writes what it was passed as an argument to standard out. Although this is a basic "Hello World" recipe, you can easily see how this 'simple' command can be used for rapid tracking of the location within a procedure, where a problem may have arisen. Add in variable values and some error handling and you can rapidly isolate issues and correct them without the additional efforts of creating a Dialog Window or writing to an error log.

Mathematical expressions

The `expr` command is used to evaluate mathematical expressions. This command can address everything from simple addition and subtraction to advanced computations, such as sine and cosine. This eliminates the need to make system calls to perform advanced mathematical functions. The `expr` command evaluates the input and arguments, and returns an integer or floating-point value.

A Tcl expression consists of a combination of operators, operands, and parenthetical containers (parenthesis, braces, or brackets). There are no strict typing requirements, so any white space is stripped by the command automatically. Tcl supports non-numeric and string comparisons as well as Tcl-specific operators.

Tcl expr operands

Tcl operands are treated as integers, where feasible. They may be specified as decimal, binary (first two characters must be 0b), hexadecimal (first two characters must be 0x), or octal (first two characters must be 0o). Care should be taken when passing integers with a leading 0, for example 08, as the interpreter would evaluate 08 as an illegal octal value. If no integer formats are included, the command will evaluate the operand as a floating-point numeric value. For scientific notations, the character e (or E) is inserted as appropriate. If no numeric interpretation is feasible, the value will be evaluated as a string. In this case, the value must be enclosed within double quotes or braces. Please note that not all operands are accepted by all operators. To avoid inadvertent variable substitution, it is always best to enclose the operands within braces. For example, take a look at the following:

- `expr 1+1*3` will return a value of `4`.
- `expr (1+1)*3` will return a value of `6`.

Operands may be presented in any of the following:

Operand	Explanation
Numeric	Integer and floating-point values may be passed directly to the command.
Boolean	All standard Boolean values (true, false, yes, no, 0, or 1) are supported.
Tcl variable	All referenced variables (in Tcl, a variable is referenced using the `$` notation, for example, `myVariable` is a named variable, whereas `$myVariable` is the referenced variable).
Strings (in double quotes)	Strings contained within double quotes may be passed with no need to include backslash, variable, or command substitution, as these are handled automatically (see the chapter on *String Expressions and Handling* for clarification on these terms and their usage).
Strings (in braces)	Strings contained within braces will be used with no substitution.
Tcl commands	Tcl commands must be enclosed within square braces. The command will be executed and the mathematical function is performed on the return value.
Named functions	Functions, such as sine, cosine, and so on.

Tcl supports a subset of the C programming language math operators and treats them in the same manner and precedence. If a named function (such as sine) is encountered, `expr` automatically makes a call to the `mathfunc` namespace to minimize the syntax required to obtain the value.

Tcl `expr` operators may be specified as noted in the following table, in the descending order of precedence:

Operator	Explanation
- + ~ !	Unary minus, unary plus, bitwise NOT and logical NOT. Cannot be applied to string operands. Bit-wise NOT may be applied to only integers.
**	Exponentiation Numeric operands only.
*/ %	Multiply, divide, and remainder. Numeric operands only.
+ -	Add and subtract. Numeric operands only.

Operator	Explanation
<< >>	Left shift and right shift. Integer operands only. A right shift always propagates the sign bit.
< > <= >=	Boolean Less, Boolean Greater, Boolean Less Than or Equal To, Boolean Greater Than or Equal To (A value of 1 is returned if the condition is true, otherwise a 0 is returned). If utilized for strings, string comparison will be applied.
== !=	Boolean Equal and Boolean Not Equal (A value of 1 is returned if the condition is true, otherwise a 0 is returned).
`eq ne`	Boolean String Equal and Boolean String Not Equal (A value of 1 is returned if the condition is true, otherwise a 0 is returned). Any operand provided will be interpreted as a string.
`in ni`	List Containment and Negated List Containment (A value of 1 is returned if the condition is true, otherwise a 0 is returned). The first operand is treated as a string value, the second as a list.
&	Bitwise AND Integers only.
^	Bitwise Exclusive OR Integers only.
|	Bitwise OR Integers only.
&&	Logical `AND` (a value of 1 is returned if both operands are 0, otherwise a 1 is returned). Boolean and numeric (integer and floating-point) operands only.
x?y:z	`If-then-else` (if `x` evaluates to non-zero, then the return is the value of `y`, otherwise the value of `z` is returned). The `x` operand must have a Boolean or a numeric value.

Mathematical functions

Mathematical functions (such as sine and cosine) are replaced with a call to the Tcl `mathfunc` namespace. This does not require any additional syntax to access the namespace as it is called automatically. These are invoked by passing the Function followed by the value or values to evaluate to the expr command. Those functions that accept multiple arguments require that the arguments be comma delimited. The default Mathematical functions are listed below in alphabetical order. These functions require a specific syntax (for example `expr {function(value,value)}`) to be accessed, as described in the *Computing mathematical expressions* section that follows:

Function	Result
`abs arg`	Returns the absolute value of `arg`. Numeric operators may be integer or floating-point. Value is returned in the same format.
`acos arg`	Returns the arc cosine of `arg`.
`asin arg`	Returns the arc sine of `arg`.
`atan arg`	Returns the Arc Tangent of x/y.
`bool arg`	Returns the Boolean value of `arg` where non-numeric values are `true`, otherwise the value is `false`.
`ceil arg`	Returns the smallest floating-point integer value not less than `arg`. Any numeric value is acceptable.
`cos arg`	Returns the cosine of `arg`, measured in radians. If the result produces an over-flow, an error is returned.
`double arg`	Converts `arg` to its floating-point value. May return INF or -INF when the numeric value is such that it exceeds the floating-point value.
`entier arg`	Converts `arg` to its integer value.
`exp arg`	Returns the exponential of `arg`. If the result produces an over-flow, an error is returned.
`floor arg`	Returns the largest floating-point integer not greater than `arg`. The argument may be any numeric value.
`fmod x y`	Returns the remainder of `x/y` as a floating-point integer. If `y` is a zero (0), then an error is returned.
`hypot x y`	Returns the length of the hypotenuse of a right angled triangle.
`int arg`	Returns the low order bits of `arg` up to the machine word size.
`isqrt arg`	Returns the integer portion of the square root of `arg`. Arg must be a positive value (integer or floating-point).

Function	Result
`log arg`	Returns the natural logarithm of `arg`. `arg` must be a positive value.
`log10 arg`	Returns the base 10 logarithm of `arg`. `arg` must be a positive value.
`max arg`	This function accepts one or more numeric values and returns the greatest.
`min arg`	This function accepts one or more numeric and returns the least one.
`pow x y`	Returns the value of `x` raised to the power `y`. If `x` is zero (0), `y` must be an integer value.
`rand`	Returns a pseudo-random floating-point integer in the range of 0, 1.
`round arg`	Returns the rounded value of `arg` if `arg` is an integer value. If `arg` is not an integer, it is converted to an integer by rounding and the converted value is returned.
`sin arg`	Returns the sine of `arg` as radians.
`sinh arg`	Returns the hyperbolic sin of `arg`. If the result produces an over-flow, an error is returned.
`sqrt arg`	Returns the square root of `arg`. Accepts any non-negative numeric value. May return INF when the value is a numeric value that exceeds the square of the maximum value for the floating-point range.
`srand arg`	Resets the seed for the random number generator and returns a random number as described in `rand`.
`tan arg`	Returns the tangent of `arg` as radians.
`tanh arg`	Returns the hyperbolic tangent of `arg`.
`wide arg`	Returns the low order 64 bits of `arg`. Accepts any numeric value.

Computing mathematical expressions

In the following examples, we will see the correct syntax for both simple and complex mathematical formulas. To accomplish these computations, we will be using the Tcl `expr` command. The `expr` command, as its name implies, is used to evaluate mathematical expressions. This command can address everything from simple addition and subtraction to advanced computations such as sine and cosine. This removes the need to make system calls to perform advanced mathematical functions. The `expr` command evaluates the input and arguments and returns an integer, floating-point, or string value as appropriate.

A Tcl expression consists of a combination of operators, operands, and parenthetical containers (parenthesis, braces, or brackets). There are no strict typing requirements so any white space is stripped by the command automatically. Tcl supports non-numeric and string comparisons as well as Tcl specific operators.

As you will see, some computations may be performed without parenthetical notations; however, it is best to get into the habit of always using them. For example, `expr 1+1` and `expr (1+1)` will both return a value of `2`. While the omission of the parenthetical notation is completely acceptable in this usage of the `expr` command, I recommend developing the habit of always using them.

My personal favorite is the `if-then-else` expression. It provides a rapid method for comparison in a "single line" format. For example, if x and y are equal to 10, while z = 4 would be entered as `expr ($x?$y:$z)`. This expression evaluates `$x` as a Boolean expression. If it's true the expression will return `$y`; if it's false, it returns `$z`.

Parenthetical notation is required for any operation that will access a specific mathematical function. For example: `expr {pow (8, 4)}` will access the mathematical `power` function and return a value of 4096.

Variable substitution is handled using the Tcl `$` notation. The following example uses an `x` variable with a value of `4` and is entered as `expr {pow (8, $x)}`. This expression returns a value of 4096 as observed in the previous example. In the second case, `$x` has been processed with its variable value of `4`.

Referencing files in Tcl

Tcl commands that accept filenames as arguments require that they be in one of three formats, depending on the platform in use. The platform in use is stored in the global `TCL_platform` array variable, created at the start of the program. Please note that to address issues of portability, you must manually manipulate the formats to ensure that they are annotated correctly.

These formats are **absolute**, **relative**, and **volume-related**.

File Formats	Explanation
Absolute	Absolute names are fully qualified and give a path to the file relative to a particular volume.
Relative	Relative filenames are unqualified and give the path to the desired file relative to the current working directory.
Volume-related	Volume-related filenames are partially qualified and either accepts the path relative to the current working directory on the current volume, or relative to the directory of a specified directory.

The following conventions are platform-specific annotations for both the directory structure and the specific filenames.

UNIX (UNIX, Linux and Mac OS X)

On the UNIX style platforms, Tcl uses path names, wherein the various components are separated by the slash (/) character. Multiple adjacent slashes are handled as a single occurrence. Trailing slashes are ignored completely. For example, passwd and passwd/ both refer to the file passwd in the current directory

Convention	Meaning
.	Special character that refers to the current directory
..	Special character that refers to the parent directory
/	Root directory
`/etc/passwd`	Absolute path to the file passwd in the directory etc
`passwd`	Relative path to the file passwd in the current directory
`etc/passwd`	Relative path to the file passwd in the directory etc from the current working directory
`../passwd`	Relative path to the file passwd in the parent directory

Windows

Tcl supports both drive-related and **Universal Naming Convention** (**UNC**) file naming conventions. Both the slash (/) and backslash (\) characters may be used as separators; however, care must be exercised when utilizing the backslash characters, as they can result in undesirable effects *if* the filename is not enclosed within quotes. Drive-related filenames consist of the optional drive letter followed by the absolute or relative path. UNC filenames follow the form of `\\servername\sharename\path\file`. The UNC filename must contain the server and share components, at least.

Convention	Meaning
.	Special character that refers to the current directory
..	Special character that refers to the parent directory
`\\MyServer\MyShare\passwd`	Absolute UNC path to the file passwd on server MyServer in the share MyShare
`C:passwd`	Volume related path to the file passwd in the current directory
`C:\passwd`	Absolute path to the file passwd in the root directory of the C drive

Convention	Meaning
`\passwd`	Volume-related path to the file passwd in the root directory of the current volume.
`etc\passwd`	Volume-related path to the file passwd in the directory etc on the current volume.

In addition to the filename conventions listed in the preceding table, Tcl supports the Berkeley UNIX **C Shell** (**csh**) tilde (~) substitution. In the case of a filename with a preceding tilde, it will be interpreted by replacing the tilde with the current user's home directory. This is not platform-dependant.

Variables

As with all the programming languages, it is the variable that allows for true flexibility and usability. Tcl differs from some scripted languages, as, there is no need to implicitly declare the variable type. For example a variable of "3" will be stored within Tcl with the same internal representation, as if it have been defined as the integer 3. If the variable is then used in a calculation, Tcl will then convert it to an integer for computation. This is referred to as **shimmering** in Tcl.

Basic variable commands

Variable command	Explanation
`global var`	This command is used to declare a global variable. It is only required within the body of a procedure.
`incr var value`	This command will increment the value stored in `var` by the value provided. Value must contain an integer. If no value is passed, the command defaults to increase the value by one (1).
`set var value`	This command sets `var` to the value provided. Conversely, the value may contain a Tcl command, the results of which will be utilized as the final value. The Command must be enclosed within square braces.
`unset var var var`	The unset command deletes one or more variables. If the `-nocomplain` flag is passed as the first argument, all the errors are suppressed. Variable names are NOT comma delimited.

In the following examples, we will create a variable with an integer value of 3, increment that value, and then delete the variable.

Getting Ready

To complete the following examples, launch your Tcl Shell as appropriate, based on your operating platform.

How to do it...

For setting a variable, enter the following command:

```
% set x 3
3
```

How it works...

The set command returns `3` to confirm that the value was set correctly.

There's more...

Enter the following command:

```
% incr x 3
6
```

The `incr` command has increased the value of `x` by `3` and returned `6`.

Unsetting a variable

Enter the following command:

```
% unset x
%
```

The `unset` command deletes the variable `x` and simply returns to the command prompt.

If the named variable does not exist, an error will be generated, as shown in the following example:

```
% unset y
can't unset "y": no such variable
```

To avoid error reporting for variables, include the `-nocomplain` switch, as illustrated here:

```
% unset -nocomplain y
%
```

In this instance, the `unset` command has ignored the error and simply returned to the command line. This is invaluable when passing a list of variables to `unset` to ensure non-existing variables do not generate an error. Additionally, you should insert -- (double minus, no spaces) after all the options, in order to remove a variable that has the same name as the many options.

Command line arguments

With any scripting language, the ability to provide arguments allows you to write a script that accepts arguments to perform a specific function.

As previously discussed, Tcl has several global variables to allow for the passing of command line arguments. The number of command line arguments to a Tcl script is passed as the global variable `argc`. The name of a Tcl script is passed to the script as the global variable `argv0`, and the arguments are passed as a list in the `argv` global variable.

Launching a Tcl script

In the following example we will invoke a Tcl script contained within a text file. This script will accept any number of arguments and print out the script name, the count of the arguments and the values contained within the `argv` variable.

Getting Ready

To complete the following example we will need to create a Tcl script file in your working directory. Open your text editor of choice and follow the instructions below.

How to do it...

Create a text file named `args.tcl` that contains the following commands.

```
# If no command line arguments are passed perform no actions
if {$argc > 0} {
# Print out the filename of the script
puts "The name of the script is: $argv0"
# Print out the count of the arguments passed
puts "Total count of arguments passed is: $argc"
# Print out a list of the arguments
puts "The arguments passed are: $argv"
# Using the List Index of argv print a specific argument
puts "The first argument passed was [lindex $argv 0]"
}
```

After you have created the file invoke the script with the following command line:

```
% Tclsh85 args.Tcl ONE 2 3
The name of the script is: args.Tcl
Total count of arguments passed is: 3
The arguments passed are: ONE 2 3
The first argument passed was ONE
%
```

How it works...

As you can see, the script accepts any number of arguments and using the Tcl global variables allows access to the arguments passed as either a list or individual values. Keep in mind that when passing control characters, they must be escaped using the backslash character.

There's more...

Invoke the script with the following command line:

```
% Tclsh85 args.Tcl \home \etc
The name of the script is: args.Tcl
Total count of arguments passed is: 2
The arguments passed are: home etc
The first argument passed was home
%
```

In the above example you can see that the backslash characters are removed. This is NOT done by Tcl, but rather by the shell from which Tcl was invoked.

Now invoke the script with the escape character added:

```
% Tclsh85 args.Tcl \\home \\etc
The name of the script is: args.Tcl
Total count of arguments passed is: 2
The arguments passed are: {\home} {\etc}
The first argument passed was \home
%
```

By adding the escape character the backslash characters are retained and curly braces have been appended to define the values as strings. For UNC file paths that contain double backslash characters you would need to enter one escape character for each backslash for a total of four. You may also 'protect' the data by enclosing it within quotes, however this is a feature of the shell used to invoke Tcl and not the Tcl shell.

2

Using the Building Blocks Control Constructs

In this chapter, we will cover:

- Looping with `if`
- Looping with `for`
- Looping with `foreach`
- Looping with `while`
- Continuing a procedure
- Breaking out of a procedure
- Nested looping

Introduction

Control constructs are the building blocks of an action. In this chapter, we will explore the creation of procedures, as well as managing the flow of events.

Prior to the creation of constructs the programmer's primary tool was the `goto` statement. While this allowed recursive handling of conditions and minimized impact on memory usage, it resulted in non-modular code and added substantially to the overhead of debugging and maintenance.

In Tcl, as in all programming languages, a control construct is a command that instructs the program to perform a certain action (or actions) based on a predefined condition. How many times the action (or actions) is/are performed is based on the specific construct used. For example, an `if` statement will perform the pre-defined actions once, whereas a `while` statement will perform the actions until the condition is no longer met.

Tcl has a full contingent of control constructs. The basic usages or descriptions of these commands are as follows:

- `if`

  The syntax for `if` command is as follows:

  `if [condition 1] then [body1] elseif [condition 2] else [body2]`
  Multiple `elseif` and `then` statements may be added as required.

- `for`

  The syntax for the `for` command is as follows:

  `for [start] [test] (next) [body]`

- `foreach`

  The syntax for the `foreach` command is as follows:

  `foreach [varlist] [valuelist] [action]`

- `while`

  The syntax for `while` command is as follows:

  `while [condition] [action]`

- `continue`

  Typically, the `continue` command is invoked from within the body of a control construct such as a `for`, `foreach`, or `while`. The `continue` command stops processing the current action and proceeds to the next iteration of the containing construct.

- `break`

  Typically, the `break` command is invoked from within the body of a control construct such as a `for`, `foreach`, or `while`. The `break` command terminates processing of the script out to the innermost containing loop of the construct.

In the following examples, I will discuss the various control constructs in detail. To illustrate the differences better, all of the examples—with the exception of the `if` command—will result in similar, and in many cases, an identical output. This was done to demonstrate how the constructs interact with the values provided. To complete each of the following examples, you will need to create a Tcl script file in your working directory. To accomplish this, you will open the text editor of your choice and follow the instructions in each section.

Controlling flow with the if statement

The `if` command evaluates a condition and if the condition evaluates to true, the actions are performed. The condition must be Boolean. With the addition of the `else` and `elseif` keywords, multiple conditions may be evaluated and numerous actions can be performed.

How to do it...

In the following recipe, we will create a Tcl script to be called from the command line that evaluates the argument passed, and based on the argument provided, perform an action.

Create a text file named `if.tcl` that contains the following commands:

```
# Set the variable x to the argument
set x [lindex $argv 0]
# Test for condition 1
if {$x == 1} {
puts "Condition 1 - You entered: $x"
# Test for condition 1
} elseif {$x == 2} {
   puts "Condition 2 - You entered: $x"
# If neither condition is met perform the default action
} else {
   puts "$x is not a valid argument"
}
```

Now invoke the script using the following command line:

```
tclsh85 if.tcl 1
Condition 1 - You entered: 1
```

How it works...

The `if` command has evaluated the argument passed; based on the argument value passed, it has evaluated the argument. As condition `1` was met, the first action was performed.

There's more...

Now invoke using the following command line:

```
tclsh85 if.tcl 2
You entered: 2
```

As condition 2 was met, the second action was performed.

Now invoke using the following command line:

tclsh85 if.tcl x

x is not a valid argument

The if construct also provides the then keyword. When using multiple conditions, the then keyword can optionally be used for clarity, as you can see in the following example:

```
if {
  $x in {1 2 3}
} then {
  puts "$x"
}
```

Try rewriting the if.tcl script using multiple conditional statements.

Looping with for

The for command performs the actions desired as long as the condition is met. In this manner the condition is repeatedly evaluated and the actions are performed as long as the condition remains true. The syntax of the for statement consists of three arguments (start, test, and next) and a body:

```
for start test next body
```

The start, next, and the body arguments must be in the form of Tcl command strings with test as an expression string. The for command invokes the interpreter to execute start. Then, it repeatedly evaluates test as an expression. While the result is non-zero, it invokes the Tcl interpreter on body. Then, it invokes the interpreter on next and repeats the loop. The command terminates when test is evaluated to 0.

Please note that the condition should always be enclosed within braces to avoid command substitution prior to processing, which may result in the dreaded infinite loop.

How to do it...

In the following recipe, we will create a Tcl script to be called from the command line that increments the value of x and prints out the value.

Create a text file named for.tcl that contains the following commands.

```
# While x is less than 11 print out the value of x
for {set x 1} {$x < 11} {incr x} {
    puts "x = $x"
}
```

Now invoke the script using the following command line:

```
tclsh85 for.tcl
x = 1
x = 2
x = 3
x = 4
x = 5
x = 6
x = 7
x = 8
x = 9
x = 10
```

How it works...

As you can see, the action was invoked multiple times while the condition remained true. As we wanted to start at 1 and print out up to 10, the condition was set to be true while `x` was less than 11. This could have been done by setting the condition to <=10 (less than or equal to 10) as well.

Looping with foreach

The `foreach` command implements a loop with the variable or variables assigned values from one or more lists and then performs an action. The list or lists may be pre-existing or created as part of the command. This command allows us to perform actions on a list or list of values with minimal effort.

How to do it...

In the following recipe, we will create a Tcl script, to be called from the command line, that recreates the previous recipe by providing hard coded values.

Create a text file named `foreach.tcl` that contains the following commands.

```
# First we create a list containing the values to print
set numbers {1 2 3 4 5 6 7 8 9 10}
foreach x $numbers {
puts "x = $x"
}
```

Now invoke the script using the following command line:

```
% tclsh85 foreach.tcl
x = 1
x = 2
x = 3
x = 4
x = 5
x = 6
x = 7
x = 8
x = 9
x = 10
```

How it works...

The action was invoked a total of 10 times as in the previous example. However, as we provided a list to be used, there was no computation required. This is exceptionally valuable for the manipulation of list data, previously created as a part of a larger program.

Looping with while

The `while` command implements a loop and applies the action as long as the condition remains true, as seen in the `for` command example. However, as the `while` command provides looping functionality, the action is repeated numerous times, as in the `foreach` command.

How to do it...

In the following recipe, we will create a Tcl script, to be called from the command line, that increments the value of `x` and prints out the value as in the `for` command recipe.

Create a text file named `while.tcl` that contains the following commands:

```
set x 1
while {$x < 11} {
    puts "x = $x"
    incr x
}
```

Now invoke the script using the following command line:

```
tclsh85 while.tcl
x = 1
x = 2
x = 3
x = 4
x = 5
x = 6
x = 7
x = 8
x = 9
x = 10
```

How it works...

The action was invoked a total of 10 times as in the previous example.

Continuing a procedure

While the `continue` keyword is not a control construct in itself, it allows you to affect the control flow.

How to do it...

In the following recipe, we will create a Tcl script, to be called from the command line, that increments the value of `x` and prints out the value as in the `for` command recipe. However, the output will be skipped when `x` is equal to 5.

Create a text file named `continue.tcl` that contains the following commands.

Please note that within the comparison used to invoke the `continue` keyword, I have added a blank line for clarification. This is not needed for the `continue` statement but does make the output more legible as well as illustrating the usage of conditional check to perform additional actions.

```
for {set x 1} {$x < 11} {incr x} {
   if {$x == 5} {
      puts " "
      continue
   }
   puts "x = $x"
}
```

Now invoke the script using the following command line:

```
% tclsh85 continue.tcl
x = 1
x = 2
x = 3
x = 4

x = 6
x = 7
x = 8
x = 9
x = 10
```

How it works...

The action was invoked 10 times, as in the previous example. However, with the addition of the `continue` keyword, we were able to skip the output for the undesired value.

Breaking out of a procedure

As with the `continue` keyword, `break` is not in and of itself a control construct. The `break` keyword allows you to terminate the processing of a loop, whenever a specific condition is encountered. I routinely use this as a method of avoiding an endless loop by setting a maximum value to be detected and to break out of the loop.

How to do it...

In the following recipe, we will create a Tcl script, to be called from the command line, that increments the value of `x` and without the `break` keyword, would create the endless loop as mentioned. Once the upper limit has been reached the loop will break and the output will be an error message.

Create a text file named `break.tcl` that contains the following commands:

```
for {set x 1} {$x > 0} {incr x} {
   if {$x == 5} {
      puts "Upper limit reached"
      break
   }
   puts "x = $x"
}
```

Now invoke the script using the following command line:

```
% tclsh85 break.tcl
x = 1
x = 2
x = 3
x = 4
Upper limit reached
```

How it works...

The action was invoked a total of five times, due to the inclusion of the `break` command. Without the `break` command, it would have continued merrily on its way, until it hit the maximum integer value for your platform.

Nested looping

Nesting of control constructs provides a valuable method for ensuring that you are acting on the values desired, as well as combining multiple actions, within the same portion of the code. In this section, we will be expanding on that premise to illustrate the nesting of different control constructs within the same script.

How to do it...

In the following recipe, we will create a Tcl script, that accepts two numeric arguments (`x` and `y`), where `y` is greater than `x`, evaluates the existence of the arguments, and prints out the values between `x` and `y`.

Create a text file named `nest.tcl` that contains the following commands:

```
if {$argc == 2} {
  set x [lindex $argv 0]
  set y [lindex $argv 1]
  puts "Beginning the while loop"
  for {set i $x} {$i <= $y} {incr i} {puts $i}
} else {
  puts "Invalid number of arguments"
}
```

Now invoke the script using the following command line:

```
% tclsh85 nest.tcl 1
Invalid number of arguments
```

How it works...

As you can see by the output, the `\if` statement evaluated as false and the inner loop was never reached.

There's more...

Now invoke the script using the following command line:

```
% tclsh85 nest.tcl 5 10
5
6
7
8
9
10
```

In this instance, we have entered the `for` loop and invoked the actions until our upper limit was reached.

3

Error Handling

In this chapter, we will cover:

- Using the `catch` command
- Using the `eval` command
- Using the `error` command
- Error handling procedure

Introduction

As discussed in the introduction to this book, I eventually learned the true power of the Tcl shell and how it can be used to locate and diagnose issues within the code. By using the `puts` statement I was able to track changes in variables and isolate sections of the code that were presenting issues.

In this chapter we will investigate the commands built into the Tcl shell that allow for more elegant error handling and isolation of sections of code to ensure that they perform correctly before proceeding with a procedure.

Error handling within Tcl allows the developer the freedom to determine how to react to an error. In the following sections we will explore Tcl error handling by implementing these control constructs to illustrate how you can use error handling to proceed with the command without raising an error or returning a Tcl error code. Based on which error handling command you decide to use, you can react accordingly and present the end user with the desired result.

The error handling constructs are as follows:

Control construct	Explanation
`catch`	`catch` script result `optionalVarName`. The `catch` command will evaluate a script and trap all exceptional returns. It the `optionalVarName` is provided it is set to the result of the evaluation.
`eval`	`eval` argument. The `eval` command accepts one or more arguments that comprise a Tcl script containing one or more commands. Returns the result of the evaluation.
`error`	`error` message information code. The error command generates an error and is used to create the messages to be logged or returned to the end user.

By using error handling control constructs, we can not only determine in advance if an error might occur, but also present the end user with information or instructions on how to proceed.

Using the catch command

The `catch` construct is used to prevent errors from aborting a script. The `catch` construct is a method of isolating errors and allowing you to determine how to proceed. This allows you to present the end user with a customized notification, as opposed to a system-defined error message, which may have no meaning to the user.

In the event an error condition exists, the `catch` command returns a non-zero integer value corresponding to the Tcl return code. Tcl provides four exceptional return codes. A return value of 1 (`TCL_ERROR`) indicates that an error has occurred and the value is stored in the result. A return of 2 (`TCL_RETURN`) is generated by the `return` command. A return of 3 (`TCL_BREAK`) is generated by the `break` command. A return of 4 (`TCL_CONTINUE`) is returned by the `continue` command.

If the `optionalVarName` is provided, it will be set to a dictionary containing the return values. This dictionary (see *Chapter 6* for further information on the Tcl Dictionary data type) will always contain two entries at least: `-code` (this will be the same as the return code) and `-level`. For more information on level, see the return section in the command list.

When an error exists three additional entries are defined within the dictionary. These are `-errorinfo`, `-errorcode`, and `-errorline`. The `-errorinfo` will contain a stack trace containing the information of the error. The `-errorcode` is additional information on the error stored in a list. The `-errorline` entry is an integer representing the line of the script where the error occurred.

Getting ready

To complete the following example, we will need to create a Tcl script file in your working directory. Open the text editor of your choice and follow the instructions given next.

How to do it...

In the following example, we will prompt the user for a numeric value to be doubled. If an incorrect value is provided, the script will generate an error. Using the editor of your choice, create a text file named `catch.tcl` that contains the following commands:

```
# Prompt the user for a number
puts -nonewline "Enter a number: "
# Clear standard out
flush stdout
# Assign the argument to a variable (value)
gets stdin value
# Return a doubled value or error message
if {[catch {set doubled [expr $value * 2]} errmsg]} {
puts "Script Failed - $errmsg"
} else {
puts "$value doubled is: $doubled"
}
puts "Regardless of error the script continues..."
```

After you have created the file, invoke the script with the following command line:

```
% tclsh85 catch.tcl
Enter a number: 2
2 doubled is: 4
Regardless of error the script continues
```

How it works...

As you can see the script accepted the numeric value of `2` and processed it successfully. On completion of the computation the script continued.

Now invoke the script with the following command line:

```
% tclsh85 catch.tcl
Enter a number: bad_data
Script Failed - invalid bareword "bad_data"
in expression "bad_data * 2";
```

```
should be "$bad_data" or "{bad_data}" or "bad_data(...)" or ...
Regardless of error the script continues.
%
```

In this instance, the script was unable to double the value of `bad_data`. Please note that the error message not only indicates an error, but also suggests the acceptable values to correct the problem.

Using the eval command

The `eval` command accepts one or more arguments that, when combined, create a Tcl script. When invoked, it passes the stored script to the command interpreter and behaves as a normal command, returning the values or errors that may have resulted.

Although the `eval` command is not an error handling construct in itself, it provides an elegant methodology for utilizing Tcl commands as variables themselves. This allows greater freedom for passing commands to procedures and constructs, for example the error handling constructs referenced here.

Getting ready

To complete the following example, we will need to access Tcl from the command line. Launch the Tcl shell appropriately for your operating system and follow the given instructions.

How to do it...

In addition to allowing the return of the error within the return value, any script can be stored and evaluated using the `eval` command. In the following example, we will use the `eval` command combined with the `exec` command to call a system program. In this example, we will use Notepad, the Windows program. For other operating systems, please enter any program that exists within your path. Enter the following into your Tcl command line:

```
% set command {puts "Hello world"}
puts "Hello World"
% eval $command
% Hello World
```

How it works...

The `eval` command has passed the command defined to the interpreter and executed the `puts`.

There's more...

At this point, you should see Notepad (or the program you selected running). Now add a filename after the `eval` statement to pass this argument to the command.

```
% set command {exec notepad}
exec notepad
% eval $command catch.tcl
```

By employing the `eval` command, you can isolate scripts into a variable and evaluate the script in its entirety. Encasing the `eval` command into a `catch` statement to determine the success is a very effective means of trapping errors at the time they occur and avoiding program failure or, inadvertently, accepting incorrect or undesirable values in your scripts.

Using the error command

The primary usage of the `error` command is to programmatically raise an error. This allows you to interrupt the interpreter at the desired point and to present the user with an error message of your choice.

Getting ready

To complete the following example, we will need to create a Tcl script file in your working directory. Open the text editor of your choice and follow the given instructions.

How to do it...

In the following example, to illustrate, we will generate an error and a supporting error message in a location where it should *not* occur. Using the editor of your choice, create a text file named `error.tcl` that contains the following commands:

```
if {1+1==2} {
error "My Error"
}
```

After you have created the file, invoke the script with the following command line:

```
% tclsh85 error.tcl
My Error
    while executing
"error "My Error""
    invoked from within
"if {1+1==2} {
```

```
   error "My Error"
}"
    (file "error.tcl" line 1)
child process exited abnormally
%
```

How it works...

As you can see, in the command line output, we generated an error message (`My Error`) as well as the Tcl error messaging; although there was no error in the math function. While this is an unrealistic implementation, it illustrates the ability to raise an error at the desired point, with the message of your choice.

Error handling procedure

In this section, we will build an error handling procedure to expand on the catch construct example presented earlier. This recipe will accept a filename and a program name. If the file exists and can be opened for reading it will attempt to open the file within the program passed. If the file can be opened but the program fails for any other reason we will display an error message of our own creation.

Getting ready

To complete the following example we will need to create a Tcl script file in your working directory. Open the text editor of your choice and follow the given instructions.

How to do it...

Using the editor of your choice, create a text file named `error_handling.tcl` that contains the following commands:

```
#Check that two arguments were passed
if { $argc == 2 } {
   #Define variables for the filename, program
   set fname [lindex $argv 0]
   set progname [lindex $argv 1]
   #Check that the file exists for reading
   set retval [file readable $fname]
   #If the file exists for reading we will open it with the desired
program
   if {$retval !=1} {
      puts "The file $fname is not available"
```

```
    } else {
       # Attempt to open the file
       set status 0
       if {[catch {exec $progname $fname &} results options]} {
          # Obtain the dictionary values for the error
          set details [dict get $options -errorcode]
          set status [lindex $details 2]
          # Display the error message
          puts "$progname: $status"
       }
    }
} else {
  puts "This program requires two arguments - Filename and
ProgramName"
}
```

Now call the script with the following command line replacing notepad if that is not a valid program for your operating system:

```
% tclsh85 error_handling.tcl catch.tcl notepad
%
```

How it works...

Our error handling procedure has evaluated the passed argument. It was provided a valid argument and located a readable file. Based on this, it has proceeded to call the executable file and load the desired file.

Call the script a second time with the following command line:

```
% tclsh85 error_handling.tcl nofile notepad
The file nofile is not available
%
```

As you can see, notepad (or the text editor of your choice) was not launched, as a readable file did not exist.

Now call the script with the following command line:

```
% tclsh85 error_handling.tcl catch.tcl noprogram
noprogram: no such file or directory
```

The `catch` construct allowed us to trap the error and present the enduser with an error message of our choice.

4
Handling String Expressions

In this chapter, we will cover:

- Appending to a string
- Formatting a string
- Matching a regular expression within a string
- Performing character substitution on a string
- Parsing a string using conversion specifiers
- Determining the length of a string
- Comparing strings
- Comparing a string of characters
- Locating the first instance of a character
- Locating the index of a character
- Determining the class of a string
- Locating the last instance of a string
- Determining the size of a string
- Replacing values within a string
- Locating a pattern within a string
- Returning a range of characters from a string
- Creating a string of repeated characters
- Replacing ranges of characters contained within a string
- Creating a reverse string

- Converting a string to lowercase
- Converting a string to title
- Converting a string to uppercase
- Trimming a string
- Trimming leading whitespace
- Trimming trailing whitespace
- Locating the word end
- Locating the word start
- Performing variable substitution

Introduction

When I first started using Tcl, everything I read or researched stressed the mantra "Everything is a string". Coming from a hard-typed coding environment, I was used to declaring variable types and in Tcl this was not needed. A `set` command could—and still does—create the variable and assigns the type on the fly. For example, `set variable "7"` and `set variable 7` will both create a variable containing `7`. However, with Tcl, you can still print the variable containing a numeric `7` and add `1` to the variable containing a string representation of `7`.

It still holds true today that everything in Tcl is a string. When we explore the Tk Toolkit and widget creation, you will rapidly see that widgets themselves have a set of string values that determine their appearance and/or behavior.

As a pre-requisite for the recipes in this chapter, launch the Tcl shell as appropriate for your operating system. You can access Tcl from the command line to execute the commands.

As with everything else we have seen, Tcl provides a full suite of commands to assist in handling string expressions. However due to the sheer number of commands and subsets, I won't be listing every item individually in the following section. Instead we will be creating numerous recipes and examples to explore in the following sections. Please refer to the *Tcl/Tk Commands* listing at the end of this book. A general list of the commands is as follows:

Command	Description
`string`	The string command contains multiple keywords (see the section covering the command) allowing for manipulation and data gathering functions.
`append`	Appends to a string variable.
`format`	Format a string in the same manner as C `sprint`.
`regexp`	Regular expression matching.
`regsub`	Performs substitution, based on Regular expression matching.

Command	Description
`scan`	Parses a string using conversion specifiers in the same manner as C `sscanf`.
`subst`	Perform backslash, command, and variable substitution on a string.

Using the commands listed in the table, a developer can address all their needs as applies to strings. In the following sections, we will explore these commands as well as many subsets of the `string` command.

Appending to a string

Creating a string in Tcl using the `set` command is the starting point for all string commands. This will be the first command for most, if not all of the following recipes. As we have seen previously, entering a `set` variable value on the command line does this. However, to fully implement strings within a Tcl script, we need to interact with these strings from time to time, for example, with an open channel to a file or HTTP pipe. To accomplish this, we will need to read from the channel and append to the original string.

To accomplish appending to a string, Tcl provides the `append` command. The `append` command is as follows:

```
append variable value value value…
```

How to do it…

In the following example, we will create a string of comma-delimited numbers using the `for` control construct. Return values from the commands are provided for clarity. Enter the following command:

```
% set var 0
0

% for {set x 1} {$x<=10}{$x<=10} {incr x} {
append var , $x
}
%puts $var

0,1,2,3,4,5,6,7,8,9,10
```

How it works...

The `append` command accepts a named variable to contain the resulting `string` and a space delimited list of strings to append. As you can see, the `append` command accepted our variable argument and a string containing the comma. These values were used to append to original variable (containing a starting value of `0`). The resulting string output with the `puts` command displays our newly appended variable complete with commas.

Formatting a string

Strings, as we all know, are our primary way of interacting with the end user. Whether presented in a message box or simply directed to the Tcl shell, they need to be as fluid as possible, in the values they present. To accomplish this, Tcl provides the `format` command. This command allows us to format a string with variable substitution in the same manner as the ANSI C `sprintf` procedure. The `format` command is as follows:

```
format string argument argument argument…
```

The `format` command accepts a string containing the value to be formatted as well as `%` conversion specifiers. The arguments contain the values to be substituted into the final string. Each conversion specifier may contain up to six sections—an XPG2 position specifier, a set of flags, minimum field width, a numeric precision specifier, size modifier, and a conversion character. The conversion specifiers are as follows:

Specifier	Description
`d` or `i`	For converting an integer to a signed decimal string.
`u`	For converting an integer to an unsigned decimal string.
`o`	For converting an integer to an unsigned octal string.
`x` or `X`	For converting an integer to an unsigned hexadecimal string. The lowercase x is used for lowercase hexadecimal notations. The uppercase `X` will contain the uppercase hexadecimal notations.
`c`	For converting an integer to the Unicode character it represents.
`s`	No conversion is performed.
`f`	For converting the number provided to a signed decimal string of the form xxx.yyy, where the number of ys is determined with the precision of six decimal places (by default).
`e` or `E`	If the uppercase E is used, it is utilized in the string in place of the lowercase e.

Specifier	Description
g or G	If the exponent is less than -4 or greater than or equal to the precision, then this is used for converting the number utilized for the %e or %E; otherwise for converting in the same manner as %f.
%	The % sign performs no conversion; it merely inserts a % character into the string.

There are three differences between the Tcl format and the ANSI C `sprintf` procedure:

- The `%p` and `%n` conversion switches are not supported.
- The `%` conversion for `%c` *only* accepts an integer value.
- Size modifiers are ignored for formatting of floating-point values. See the full description of the format command in *Chapter 13*, the *Tcl/Tk Commands* section for the details on size modifiers.

How to do it...

In the following example, we format a long date string for output on the command line. Return values from the commands are provided for clarity. Enter the following command:

```
% set month May
May

% set weekday Friday
Friday

% set day 5
5

% set extension th
th

%set year 2010
2010

%puts [format "Today is %s, %s %d%s %d" $weekday $month $day $extension
$year]
Today is Friday, May 5th 2010
```

How it works...

The `format` command successfully replaced the desired conversion flag delimited regions with the variables assigned.

Matching a regular expression within a string

Regular expressions provide us with a powerful method to locate an arbitrarily complex pattern within a string. The `regexp` command is similar to a **Find** function in a text editor. You search for a defined string for the character or the pattern of characters you are looking for and it returns a Boolean value that indicates success or failure and populates a list of optional variables with any matched strings. The `-indices` and `-inline` options must be used to modify the behavior, as indicated by this statement. But it doesn't stop there; by providing switches, you can control the behavior of `regexp`. The switches are as follows:

Switch	Behavior
`-about`	No actual matching is made. Instead `regexp` returns a list containing information about the regular expression where the first element is a subexpression count and the second is a list of property names describing various attributes about the expression.
`-expanded`	Allows the use of expanded regular expression, wherein whitespaces and comments are ignored.
`-indices`	Returns a list of two decimal strings, containing the indices in the string to match for the first and last characters in the range.
`-line`	Enables the newline-sensitive matching similar to passing the `-linestop` and `-lineanchor` switches.
`-linestop`	Changes the behavior of [^] bracket expressions and the "." character so that they stop at newline characters.
`-lineanchor`	Changes the behavior of ^ and $ (anchors) so that they match both the beginning and end of a line.
`-nocase`	Treats uppercase characters in the search string as lowercase.
`-all`	Causes the command to match as many times as possible and returns the count of the matches found.
`-inline`	Causes `regexp` to return a list of the data that would otherwise have been placed in match variables. Match variables may NOT be used if `-inline` is specified.
`-start`	Allows us to specify a character index from which searching should start.
`--`	Denotes the end of switches being passed to `regexp`. Any argument following this switch will be treated as an expression, even if they start with a "-".

Now that we have a background in switches, let's look at the command:

```
regexp switches expression string submatchvar submatchvar...
```

The `regexp` command determines if the expression matches part or all of the string and returns a `1` if the match exists or a `0` if it is not found. If the variables (`submatchvar`) (for example `myNumber` or `myData`) are passed after the string, they are used as variables to store the returned `submatchvar`. Keep in mind that if the `-inline` switch has been passed, no return variables should be included in the command.

Getting ready

To complete the following example, we will need to create a Tcl script file in your working directory. Open the text editor of your choice and follow the next set of instructions.

How to do it...

A common use for `regexp` is to accept a string containing multiple words and to split it into its constituent parts. In the following example, we will create a string containing an IP address and assign the values to the named variables. Enter the following command:

```
% regexp "(\[0-9]{1,3})\.(\[0-9]{1,3})\.(\[0-9]{1,3})\.(\[0-9]{1,3})" \
  $ip all first second third fourth
% puts "$all \n$first \n$second \n$third \n$fourth"
192.168.1.65
192
168
1
65
```

How it works...

As you can see, the IP Address has been split into its individual octet values. What `regexp` has done is match the groupings of decimal characters [0-9] of a varying length of 1 to 3 characters {1, 3} delimited by a "." character. The original IP address is assigned to the first variable (`all`) while the octet values are assigned to the remaining variables (`first`, `second`, `third`, and `fourth`).

Performing character substitution on a string

If regexp is a Find function, then regsub is equivalent to Find and Replace. The regsub command accepts a string and using Regular Expression pattern matching, it locates and, if desired, replaces the pattern with the desired value. The syntax of regsub is similar to regexp as are the switches. However, additional control over the substitution is added. The switches are as listed next:

Switch	Description
-all	Causes the command to perform substitution for each match found The & and \n sequences are handled for each substitution
-expanded	Allows use of expanded regular expression wherein whitespace and comments are ignored
-line	Enables newline-sensitive matching similar to passing the -linestop and -lineanchor switches
-linestop	Changes the behavior of [^] bracket expressions so that they stop at newline characters
-lineanchor	Changes the behavior of ^ and $ (anchors) so that they match both the beginning and end of a line
-nocase	Treats uppercase characters in the search string as lowercase
-start	Allows specification of a character offset in the string from which to start matching

Now that we have a background in switches as they apply to the regsub command, let's look at the command:

```
regsub switches expression string substitution variable
```

The regsub command matches the expression against the string provided and either copies the string to the variable or returns the string if a variable is not provided. If a match is located, the portion of the string that matched is replaced by substitution. Whenever a substitution contains an & or a \0 character, it is replaced with the portion of the string that matches the expression. If the substitution contains the switch "\n" (where n represents a numeric value between 1 and 9), it is replaced with the portion of the string that matches with the nth sub-expression of the expression. Additional backslashes may be used in the substitution to prevent interpretation of the &, \0, \n, and the backslashes themselves. As both the regsub command and the Tcl interpreter perform backslash substitution, you should enclose the string in curly braces to prevent unintended substitution.

How to do it...

In the following example, we will substitute every instance of the word `one`, which is a word by itself, with the word `three`. Return values from the commands are provided for clarity. Enter the following command:

```
% set original "one two one two one two"
one two one two one two

% regsub -all {one} $original three new
3

% puts $new
three two three two three two
```

How it works...

As you can see, the value returned from the `regsub` command lists the number of matches found. The string `original` has been copied into the string `new`, with the substitutions completed. With the addition of additional switches, you can easily parse a lengthy string variable and perform bulk updates. I have used this to rapidly parse a large text file prior to importing data into a database.

Parsing a string using conversion specifiers

To parse a string in Tcl using conversion specifiers we will be using the `scan` command. The `scan` command parses the string in a similar manner as in the ANSI C `sscanf` procedure. As the `scan` command does not accept switches such as the `regexp` and `regsub` commands, we will proceed directly to the command. The syntax of the command is as follows:

```
scan string format variable variable variable...
```

The `scan` command accepts a string to parse and based on the format provided, it will convert the string. If variables are provided, they will be updated to the output of the conversions.

The `scan` command supports the following conversion characters:

Character	Description
d	The input string must be a decimal integer.
o	The input string must be an octal integer.

Character	Description
u	The input string must be a decimal integer (as in the case of d). The output is assigned to the variable as an unsigned decimal string.
s	The input substring consists of all the characters up to the next whitespace character.
e, f, or g	The input substring must be a floating-point number consisting of an optional sign, a string of decimals that may or may not contain a decimal point, and an optional exponentiation consisting of either an e or E followed by an optional sign and a string of decimal digits. The value is read and stored in the variable as a floating-point value.
[chars]	The input string consists of one or more characters as listed within the brackets. The matching string is stored in the variable. Note that if the first character contained within the brackets is a closed bracket, it is treated as a character. If chars contains a sequential notation of the form a-f, then any characters between a and f (a and f inclusive) will result in a match.
[^chars]	The input string consists of one or more characters *not* listed within the brackets. The matching string is stored in the variable. Note that if the first character following the ^ contained within the brackets is a closed bracket, it is treated as a character. If chars contains a sequential notation of the form a-f, then any characters between a and f (a and f inclusive) will be excluded from the match.
n	No input is accepted from the input string. Return the total number of characters scanned.

The differences between scan and the ANSI C sscanf are as follows:

- The %p conversion specifiers are unsupported
- For %c conversions, a single character value is converted to a decimal string
- If the end of the input string is reached prior to any conversion having occurred *and* no variables were provided, an empty string is returned

How to do it...

In the following example, we will parse a hexadecimal RGB color and assign the values returned to individual variables. Return values from the commands are provided for clarity. Enter the following command:

```
% set color #34aa44
#34aa44

% scan $color #%2x%2x%2x r g b
% puts "$r $g $b"
52 170 68
```

How it works...

As you can see from the example, the `scan` command accepted the hexadecimal color and returned it as its decimal equivalent to the variables provided. The `scan` command parses the sub strings from the string provided and returns the number of conversions performed (or a `-1`, if the end of the string is encountered with no conversions performed). The string provides the input to be parsed, while the format instructs the command on how to parse it using the `%` conversion specifiers. Each variable provided will receive the output of the conversion. If no variables are provided then `scan` will behave in an inline mode and return the data. If no variable is provided and no conversions occur, an empty string will be returned.

All of the remaining chapter will deal primarily with the `string` command. The various options will address most of our needs where strings occur. The `string` command is passed to the interpreter as follows:

```
string option argument argument…
```

The `string` command performs one or more operations, based on the `option` keyword or the words provided. The arguments will contain the required input and output for the specific option used. Rather than list these en masse, I will be exploring each within the following sections.

Determining the length of a string

To determine the length of a string, Tcl provides the `length` keyword. The `length` command will return a decimal string containing the number of bytes used to represent the value contained within the variable in memory. Please note that as UTF-8 uses one to three bytes for Unicode characters; the byte length will not be the same as the character length, in most circumstances. The syntax of `length` is as follows:

```
string length variable
```

How to do it...

In the following example, we will determine the byte length of a string of characters. Return values from the commands are provided for clarity. Enter the following command:

```
% set input "The end is nigh"
The end is nigh

% string length $input
15
```

How it works...

As you can see in the example, the `string` command has read the input and returned a value of `15`.

Comparing strings

In any of the programs, string comparison is critical for many reasons. To perform string comparison, Tcl provides two keywords for use with the `string` command—`compare` and `equal`. The syntax for the first keyword `compare` is as follows:

```
string compare -nocase -length string1 string2
```

When invoked with the `compare` keyword, the `string` command performs a character-by-character comparison of the strings passed in `string1` and `string2`.

The `string` command accepts two switches as mentioned here:

- `-nocase`

  Strings are compared in a case-insensitive manner
- `-length`

  Instructs the interpreter to perform the comparison only on the first length characters

Getting ready

To complete the following example, we will need to create a Tcl script file in your working directory. Open the text editor of your choice and follow the given instructions.

How to do it...

In the following example, we will create a Tcl script to accept a string value to compare against a static value. In this method, you can see the specific returns by altering the second string. Using the editor of your choice create a text file named `compare.tcl` that contains the following commands:

```
set string1 compare
set string2 [lindex $argv 0]
set output [string compare $string1 $string2]
puts $output
```

After you have created the file, invoke the script with the following command line:

```
% tclsh85 compare.tcl compare
0
```

How it works...

As it can be seen, where the return value is 0, the strings are compared and match. Try invoking this script with different arguments to see the other return values. When invoked with the `compare` keyword, it will perform a character-by-character comparison of the two strings provided. The return values are `-1`, `0`, or `1`. These indicate if the string being compared to is lexicographically less than, equal to, or greater than the comparison string. As such, the `string` command will return more information on a comparison than the simple == method.

Comparing a string of characters

The second keyword for string comparison is `equal`.

The syntax for the `string` command is as follows:

```
string equal -nocase -length int string1 string2
```

When invoked with the `equal` keyword the `string` command will perform a character-by-character comparison of the two strings provided.

The `equal` keyword accepts two switches, as follows:

- `-nocase`

  Strings are compared in a case insensitive manner
- `-length int`

  Instructs the interpreter to only perform the comparison on the first length characters

How to do it...

In the following example, we will determine if the values passed as `string1` and `string2` are equal. Return values from the commands are provided for clarity. Enter the following command:

```
% string equal Monday monday
0
```

How it works...

As you can see, the `string equal` command has compared the two strings provided and found them to not be a match. When `string` is invoked with the `equal` keyword it will perform a character-by-character comparison of the two strings provided in a similar manner as the `compare` keyword. The difference is in the return values; `equal` returns a `1` if the strings are identical or a `0` if the strings do not match.

Locating the first instance of a character

In our programs, the need to find the first occurrence of a character is not uncommon. For example, we may be parsing a large text file and need to break it up into sections, based on an instance of a character. To perform this action, the `string` command accepts the keyword `first`.

The syntax for the string command is as follows:

```
string first varString string index
```

When invoked with the `first` keyword, the `string` command will search for a character or a sequence of characters in the string. If no match is found, the command returns a `-1`. If an index is provided, the search is constrained to the match at (or after) that index within the string.

How to do it...

In the following example, we will locate the first instance of the character *a* within a string. Return values from the commands are provided for clarity. Enter the following command:

```
% string first a 123abc123abc
3
```

How it works...

As you can see, `string` has located the first instance of the character within our string value.

Locating the index of a character

What if we need to determine which character exists at a specific location within a string and not just the first instance? To accomplish this, `string`, includes the `index` keyword.

The syntax for the `string` command is as follows:

```
string index string index
```

When invoked with the `index` keyword, the `string` command returns the character that exists at the location specified in the switch. The accepted values are valid for *all* the Tcl commands that accept an index and may be passed as follows:

Value	Description
Any integer value	Integer value for a specific index. Please note that the index is 0-based.
end	The last character in the string.
end-n	The last character in the string minus the numeric offset represented by n. For example, end-2 would refer to "b" in the string "abcd".
end+n	The last character in the string plus the numeric offset represented by n.
A+B	The character located at the index, as determined by adding the values of A and B, where A and B are integer values.
A-B	The character located at the index as determined by subtracting the values of A and B where A and B are integer values.

How to do it...

In the following example we will locate the character that exists at a specific location within a string. Return values from the commands are provided for clarity. Enter the following command:

```
% string index abcde 3
d
```

How it works...

As you can see `string` has returned the character `d`, based on the index of `3`. Try the various switch values to see how they react.

Determining the class of a string

Although a string is generally considered to be an alphanumeric character, it can also belong to a class of strings. These classes allow us to manipulate the string in a manner consistent with its class type. For example, adding 1 to the character # will produce an error or unexpected return value. To assist us in determining the class of the string, Tcl provides the `is` keyword and a list of associated classes.

The syntax for the `string` command is as follows:

```
string is class -strict -failindex variable string
```

When invoked with the `is` keyword the command will return 1, if the class is matched.

The classes `is` will check for are as follows:

Class	Description
`alnum`	Any Unicode alphabetic or digit character.
`alpha`	Any Unicode alphabetic character.
`ascii`	Any character with a value less than \u0080 (those that are in the 7-bit ASCII range).
`boolean`	Any of the forms allowed by TCL_GetBoolean.
`control`	Any Unicode control character.
`digit`	Any Unicode digit character. This includes characters outside of the [0-9] range.
`double`	Any of the valid forms for a double in Tcl, with optional surrounding whitespace. In case of under/overflow in the value, 0 is returned and the `varname` will contain -1.
`false`	Any of the forms allowed to Tcl_GetBoolean where the value is false.
`graph`	Any Unicode printing character, except space.
`integer`	Any of the valid string formats for a 32-bit integer value in Tcl, with optional surrounding whitespace. In case of under/overflow in the value, 0 is returned and the `varname` will contain -1.

Class	Description
`list`	Any proper list structure, with optional surrounding whitespace. In case of improper list structure, 0 is returned and the `varname` will contain the index of the "element" where the list parsing fails or -1 if this cannot be determined.
`lower`	Any Unicode lower case alphabet character.
`print`	Any Unicode printing character, including space.
`punct`	Any Unicode punctuation character.
`space`	Any Unicode space character.
`true`	Any of the forms allowed to Tcl_GetBoolean where the value is true.
`upper`	Any upper case alphabet character in the Unicode character set.
`wideinteger`	Any of the valid forms for a wide integer in Tcl, with optional surrounding whitespace. In case of under/overflow in the value, 0 is returned and the `varname` will contain -1.
`wordchar`	Any Unicode word character. Any alphanumeric character, and any Unicode connector punctuation characters, for example an underscore.
`xdigit`	Any hexadecimal digit character ([0-9A-Fa-f]).

How to do it...

As you can see care has been taken to provide a full listing of the various classes of strings to cover all situations. In the following example we will determine if a string is a member of the `digit` class. Return values from the commands are provided for clarity. Enter the following command:

```
% string is digit a
0
```

How it works...

As you can see, `string` has returned a `0`, informing us that the character supplied is not a member of the digit class. While this is a very simple implementation of this specific keyword, it is an invaluable tool to ensure that the class desired has been provided prior to utilization. Try using various classes and string values to see the various classes and how they react when given the correct or incorrect member of a class. When invoked with the `is` keyword, the `string` command returns `1` if the class being tested for is matched, otherwise it will return a `0`. By applying the optional `-strict` switch, an empty string will return `0` as opposed to `1`. This is useful to determine the existence of an empty string. If the optional `-failindex` switch is passed and `0` is the return value, the index where the string failed the class test will be stored in variable. If the return value is `1`, the variable will not be set.

Locating the last instance of a string

To locate the last instance of a string for an exact match, Tcl provides the keyword `last`. Let's look at the syntax to illustrate how this can be used.

The syntax for the `string` command is as follows:

```
string last string1 string2 index
```

When invoked with the `last` command, the `string` command locates the last instance of `string1` contained within `string2`.

How to do it...

In the following example, we locate the last instance of a string contained within another string. Enter the following command:

```
% string last abc abcabcabc
6
```

How it works...

As you can see, `string` has returned `6`, indicating that the last exact match of the search phrase is located at the index of `6`. When invoked with the `last` keyword, the `string` command searches `string1` for a sequence of characters that exactly matches `string2`. If the match occurs, Tcl returns the index of the first letter of the occurrence. If no match exists, `-1` is returned. By passing a numeric value in the index, Tcl will commence the search at (or before) the index value.

Determining the size of a string

The size of a string can be an invaluable piece of information. Imagine if you will, loading data to a database where the field sizes are fixed at 25 characters. Trying to load a string of 50 characters into a field designed for 25 will, at best, result in a truncation of the data. Keep in mind that the byte-length of a string may be greater if multibyte characters exist. To assist us in this, Tcl has provided the `length` keyword.

The syntax of the `string` command is as follows:

```
string length string
```

The only values passed to the `string` command in this instance are the `length` keyword and the `string` to be checked.

How to do it...

In the following example, we will determine the length of a character string that contains whitespace, as you might encounter in the database scenario I mentioned earlier. The return value from the command is provided for clarity. Enter the following command:

```
% string length "123 Any Street"
14
```

How it works...

As you can see, the command has returned a value of `14` to reflect not only the alphanumeric characters, but also the enclosed whitespace.

Replacing values within a string

Tcl has added a very useful keyword to the string command to simplify alteration of the string. The `map` keyword allows us to replace values within a string as passed without having to programmatically locate the target characters.

The syntax of the `string` command is as follows:

```
string map -nocase mapping string
```

The `string` command will read the mapping provided and replace the affected values within the string. Mapping is passed as a valid Tcl list in a key-value pair format similar to that returned by performing a `get` on an array. Bear in mind that the string is only mapped once. If the optional `-nocase` switch is provided, a case insensitive match will be made.

How to do it...

In the following example, we will replace every instance of a character set inside a string. Return values from the commands are provided for clarity. Enter the following command:

```
% string map {abc def} abcabcabc
defdefdef
```

How it works...

Tcl has mapped each occurrence of the string "abc" and replaced it with the string "def".

Locating a pattern within a string

Many times, you may have the need to determine if a specific pattern exists within a string. To accomplish this, Tcl provides the `match` keyword. Let's look at the syntax and then I will explain the major differences and the real strength of this keyword.

The `string` syntax is as follows:

```
string match -nocase pattern string
```

When invoked with the `match` keyword, the `string` command will attempt to locate the pattern specified.

The following details the various methods in which the pattern can be passed and illustrates the special characters the pattern can store.

Special Characters	Description
`*`	Matches any sequence within the string, including null strings.
`?`	Matches any single character in the string.
`[characters]`	Matches any character in the set provided.
	If `chars` contains a sequential notation of the form a-f, then any characters between a and f (a and f inclusive) will result in a match.
`\x`	Matches the character specified in `x`.
	This avoids interpretation of the *, [], or \ in the pattern as special characters.

How to do it...

What these special characters allow us to accomplish is to locate a pattern within a string using wildcards and ranges. In the following example, we will determine if a specific pattern exists within a string. Return values from the commands are provided for clarity. Enter the following command:

```
% string match a??12? abc123
1
```

How it works...

Tcl has returned a value of `1` to indicate that the pattern was located. Try running this again with a single `*` instead of the double `?` characters. The `string` command scans the string provided and attempts to locate the pattern. If the pattern is located, `1` is returned; if not, the return value is `0`.

Returning a range of characters from a string

It is not uncommon to cut a string into its constituent parts. This allows the data to be stored in-line, without comma or space separation, thereby, minimizing the impact on the disk storage. To assist us in this, and other instances where we need to extract a range of characters from a string, Tcl has provided the `range` keyword.

The syntax of the `string` command is as follows:

```
string range string first last
```

When invoked with the `range` keyword, the `string` command will return all characters inclusive between those specified in the `first` and `last` location.

How to do it...

In the following example we will locate a range of characters contained within a string. Return values from the commands are provided for clarity. Enter the following command:

```
% string range abcdefg 2 4
cde
```

How it works...

As you can see, Tcl has returned the characters "cde", based on the index values passed. The `string` command returns a range of consecutive characters from the string, starting with the index value stored in `first` and ending with the value stored in `last`. An index of `0` refers to the first character. If `first` is a negative number or `last` is greater than the string length, then Tcl will adjust them to meet the actual start and end of the string.

Creating a string of repeated characters

Why would you need to create a string of identical characters? For example, to create a tabbed layout and you can't set/use tabs. To accomplish this and more Tcl has provided the `repeat` keyword to do this programmatically and saved us hours of work in the process.

The syntax of the `string` command is as follows:

```
string repeat strRepeat count
```

The `string` command will create a string containing `strRepeat` repeated `count` times.

How to do it...

In the following example we will create a string containing five identical characters. Return values from the commands are provided for clarity. Enter the following command:

```
% string repeat x 5
xxxxx
```

How it works...

As you can see, Tcl has created our string of five x characters.

Replacing ranges of characters contained within a string

Should it become necessary to replace the values stored in a string, regardless of contents, Tcl has provided the `replace` keyword.

The syntax of the `string` command is as follows:

```
string replace string first last replacement
```

How to do it...

In the following example, we will replace the characters stored in a string with new values. Return values from the commands are provided for clarity. Enter the following command:

```
% string replace abcdefg 2 5 123456789
ab123456789g
```

How it works...

Tcl has returned a new string containing the characters located within the index range, from `2` to `5`. This illustrated not only the replacement of the characters, but also the command's ability to create strings that differ in size from the original string. If your program requires that the string, when altered, should be of the same length as the original, care should be taken to avoid this alteration. The `string` command reads the value stored in `string` and replaces it with the value stored in `replacement`, based on the index values passed in `first` and `last`. Note that the replacement may increase or decrease the size of the string as needed, based on the values passed. An index of `0` refers to the first character. If `first` is a negative number or `last` is greater than the string length, then Tcl will adjust them to meet the actual start and end of the string.

Creating a reverse string

There have been instances in the past where I had the need to reverse the characters I had received from the user input. To assist us in creating a reverse string, Tcl provides the `reverse` keyword.

The syntax of the string command is as follows:

```
string reverse string
```

The `string` command returns the value stored in `string` in reverse order.

Getting ready

To complete the following example, we will need to access Tcl from the command line. Launch the Tcl shell appropriately for your operating system and follow the given instructions.

How to do it...

In the following example, we will create a string that is the reverse of the original. Return values from the commands are provided for clarity. Enter the following command:

```
% string reverse abc
cba
```

How it works...

Tcl returns a string containing the original string provided in a reverse order.

Converting a string to lowercase

To prevent the case of a string from impacting your programs, Tcl has provided several keywords to manipulate the case of stored strings. The first of these is `tolower`. As its name implies, the `tolower` keyword returns a string with all characters in lowercase.

The syntax of the `string` command is as follows:

```
string tolower string first last
```

The `string` command will convert all upper or title characters to their lowercase values and return the newly created string. If an optional index value is passed in the `first` location, the conversion will commence at that location. If an index value is passed in the `last` location, this will designate the location at which the conversion will stop.

How to do it...

In the following example, we will create a string that contains only lowercase characters. Return values from the commands are provided for clarity. Enter the following command:

```
% string tolower "NOW IS THE TIME"
now is the time
```

How it works...

As you can see Tcl has returned our lowercase string.

Converting a string to title

The second keyword that Tcl provides to alter the case of a string is `totitle`. As its name implies, the `totitle` keyword returns a string with the first Unicode character capitalized.

The syntax of the `string` command is as follows:

```
string totitle string first last
```

When invoked with the `totitle` keyword the `string` command will convert the value stored in `string` to its title equivalent.

How to do it...

In the following example, we will convert a string that contains only lowercase characters to its title case. Return values from the commands are provided for clarity. Enter the following command:

```
% string totitle "john"
John
```

How it works...

The `title` command converts the first character of a string to its Unicode title case variant. If no title variant exists, it is converted to uppercase. If an optional index value is passed in the `first` location, the conversion will commence at that location. If an index value is passed in the `last` location, this will designate the location at which the conversion will stop.

Converting a string to uppercase

The third keyword that Tcl provides to alter the case of a string is `toupper`. As its name implies, the `toupper` keyword returns a string set to all uppercase characters.

The syntax of the `string` command is as follows:

```
string toupper string first last
```

The `string` command will convert all lowercase characters in a string to uppercase. If an optional index value is passed in the `first` location, the conversion will commence at that location. If an index value is passed in the `last` location, this will designate the location at which the conversion will stop.

How to do it...

In the following example, we will convert a string that contains only lowercase characters to uppercase. Return values from the commands are provided for clarity. Enter the following command:

```
% string toupper "now is the time"
NOW IS THE TIME
```

How it works...

Tcl returns the entire string converted to its uppercase value.

Trimming a string

When writing a program, there is no way to ensure that only correctly formatted data is provided. An end-user may inadvertently enter whitespace, a test file may contain whitespaces, and so on. To address this issue, Tcl provides keywords to trim the undesirable whitespaces or characters if specified. The first of these is the `trim` keyword.

The syntax of the `string` command is as follows:

```
string trim string characters
```

If no characters are provided, the `trim` keyword will return the `string` with all leading and trailing whitespace trimmed. If the `characters` are not specified (specifying the `characters` is optional), only those whitespaces will be removed.

How to do it...

In the following example, we will trim the `.gif` extension from a string. Return values from the commands are provided for clarity. Enter the following command:

```
% string trim  "picture.gif " .gif
picture
```

How it works...

As you can see, Tcl has returned our trimmed string.

Trimming leading whitespace

The second keyword is `trimleft`. As its name implies, `trimleft` is used to trim leading whitespaces or other characters as specified.

The syntax of the `string` command is as follows:

```
string trimleft string characters
```

If no characters are provided, the `trimleft` keyword will return `string` with all leading whitespace trimmed. If the `characters` (optional) are not specified, only the whitespaces will be removed.

How to do it...

In the following example, we will trim all leading whitespace from a string. Return values from the commands are provided for clarity. Enter the following command:

```
% string trimleft "     Now is the time"
Now is the time
```

How it works...

Tcl has returned a string with all leading whitespace removed.

Trimming trailing whitespace

The third keyword is `trimright`. As its name implies, `trimright` is used to trim trailing whitespace or other characters as specified.

The syntax of the `string` command is as follows:

```
string trimright string characters
```

The `trimright` keyword will return `string` with all trailing whitespace trimmed if no characters are provided. If the optional `characters` are not specified only will be removed.

How to do it...

In the following example we will trim the trailing f characters from a string. Return values from the commands are provided for clarity. Enter the following command:

```
% string trimright  "Now is the timef " f
Now is the time
```

How it works...

Tcl has trimmed all occurrences of the character `f` from the right side of the string.

Locating the word end

In a large character string, it may become necessary to know what is the end of a word. For example, we may require this information in order to determine where to extract data for a variable. To accomplish this, Tcl has provided the `wordend` keyword.

The syntax of the `string` command is as follows:

```
string wordend string index
```

This command will return the index of the first character that immediately follows the last character of the word contained within the `string` that is located at the value passed in `index`. In Tcl, a word is any contiguous range of alphanumeric characters (for example cat, dog, 123).

How to do it...

In the following example, we will determine the end of a word contained within a string. Return values from the commands are provided for clarity. Enter the following command:

```
% string wordend "Now is the time" 2
3
```

How it works...

Tcl returns the index for the character after the end of the word "Now".

Locating the word start

While it is all well and good that we know where our word ended, what if we need to know where it starts? To accomplish this, Tcl has provided the `wordstart` keyword.

The syntax of the `string` command is as follows:

```
string wordstart string index
```

This command will return the index of the first character of the word contained within `string` that is located at the value passed in `index`.

How to do it...

In the following example, we will determine the start of a word contained within a string. Return values from the commands are provided for clarity. Enter the following command:

```
% string wordstart "Now is the time" 12
11
```

How it works...

As you can see, Tcl has returned the index for the first character of the word "time".

Performing variable substitution

Now that we have mapped, formatted, counted, analyzed, and generally picked our strings apart, let's look at programmatically performing variable substitution in a string. As Tcl always seems to do, we have been provided with a powerful command to simplify the task with the `subst` command. While you could easily invoke the `set` command to change the contents, `subst` provides the ability to alter portions of a variable by providing optional switches.

The syntax of the `subst` command is as follows:

```
subst switch string
```

The `subst` command performs variable substitution to a string. The behavior may be controlled with optional switches.

These switches are as follows:

Switch	Description
`-nobackslashes`	No backslash substitution will be performed.
`-nocommands`	No command substitution will be performed.
`-novariables`	No variable substitution will be performed.

How to do it...

In the following example, we will create a string that contains the value of a variable using the `subst` command. Return values from the commands are provided for clarity. Enter the following command:

```
% set a de

de

% subst {abc {$a}}
abc {de}
```

How it works...

Tcl has returned `abc {de}` and not `abc {$a}`. By applying the `subst` command it becomes very easy to create a string that contains control characters, backslashes, and the values we require for the return. The `subst` command will perform variable, command, and backslash substitution on `string` and return the newly created string value. Based on the switch or switches passed in at the `switch` location, specific functionality of the command may be suppressed.

5
Expanding String Functionality Using Lists

In this chapter, we will cover the following topics:

- Creating a list
- Joining two lists
- Joining list elements
- Appending list elements
- Assigning list elements to variables
- Retrieving an element from a list
- Inserting elements into a list
- Determining the number of elements
- Getting a list element
- Repeating elements
- Replacing elements
- Reversing elements
- Searching a list
- Editing a list
- Sorting a list
- Splitting a string into a list

Introduction

Now that we have a firm grasp on the string type, let's look at the Tcl command `list`. As you might have discerned from the command name, this command is used to create and manage lists of information. While the various string handling commands allow for the creation of a string containing anything from a single character to larger text files, the list allows you to create, manipulate, and utilize a list of arguments in the same manner as a shopping list. In Tcl, each of the separate items in a list are referred to as **elements**.

In the following sections, we will examine not only the creation of a list, but also the many commands provided by Tcl to allow you to fully utilize the list and its elements. As a pre-requisite for the recipes in this chapter, launch the Tcl shell appropriately for your operating system. You can access Tcl from the command line to execute the commands.

Creating a list

One way to create a list is to simply use the `list` command. Bear it in mind that with this command you must be aware of quotations. Inconsistent quotations can have unexpected results on the list elements. The syntax is as follows:

```
list value1 value2…
```

How to do it...

In the following example, we will create a list containing single characters. Return values from the commands are provided for clarity. Enter the following command:

```
% list John Mary Bill
John Mary Bill
```

How it works...

The `list` commands returns a list containing all the arguments supplied, or an empty string if no arguments are specified. Backslashes and braces are added to the string representation of the list as it is necessary to provide a properly formatted list that will work with any `list` command.

There's more...

As mentioned earlier, quotation marks can alter how items are stored in our list. In the following example, we will recreate our list; but this time the elements will be encased in quotation marks to illustrate their effect on our list. Enter the following command:

```
% list John "Mary Smith" Bill " "
John {Mary Smith} Bill { }
```

As you can see, the elements and the empty spaces enclosed within the quotation marks are returned as elements, denoted by the curly braces. In later sections, when we access specific elements, you can easily see how inadvertent or incorrect quotation usage can have an unexpected return from commands.

Joining two lists

Now that we have seen how to make a list we will explore combining lists. To accomplish this, Tcl provides the `concat` command. The syntax is as follows:

```
concat value1 value2 …
```

How to do it…

In the following example, we will concatenate a set of lists containing single characters. Return values from the commands are provided for clarity. Enter the following command:

```
% concat {a b c} {1 2 3}
a b c 1 2 3
```

How it works…

The `concat` command joins each of its arguments together with spaces after first trimming all leading and trailing whitespace, and in the case of a list, the results will be flattened. Although this command will concatenate any arguments provided, we will be focusing on its usage as it applies to the list elements. To denote that a list is being provided as the argument, it should be encased within braces {}. This is another method of providing lists. They may also be passed as named list variables, actual list commands, or within quotes. If no arguments are provided, it will return an empty string.

There's more…

In the following example, we will concatenate a list containing string values with additional string values to illustrate using `concat` to expand the elements in our list. Return values from the commands are provided for clarity. Enter the following command:

```
% concat {John Mary Bill} Tom Fred Sally
John Mary Bill Tom Fred Sally
```

As you can see in this example, the return value is a string containing not only our list but also the individual arguments provided.

Joining list elements

While the `concat` command is more than capable of merging lists and arguments into a single list, Tcl also provides the `join` command to expand the functionality. The `join` command will not only merge the arguments, but also allows insertion of a separation character into the returned string. Note that the variable provided must contain a list, set of lists, or standalone values. The syntax is as follows:

```
join list delimiter
```

How to do it…

In the following example, we will join the elements of a list and create a comma-delimited string. Return values from the commands are provided for clarity. Enter the following command:

```
% set input {John Mary Bill}
John Mary Bill

% join $input ", "
John, Mary, Bill
```

How it works…

The `join` command returns the complete string created by joining all elements of the variable provided. If a delimiter is specified, it will create a delimited list, otherwise the string will be returned space delimited.

There's more…

In the following example, we will join two lists in the same manner as the `concat` command and convert the lists into a single string value. Return values from the commands are provided for clarity. Enter the following command:

```
% set input {{John Mary Bill} {Tom Fred Sally}}
{John Mary Bill} {Tom Fred Sally}

% join $input
John Mary Bill Tom Fred Sally
```

As you can see, the `join` command has accepted the arguments and returned a string containing the elements of the two lists flattened.

Appending list elements

Up to this point, we have manually populated the elements of our list. While this is a usable method for list creation, it will become a necessity to programmatically populate the elements of a list at some point. To accomplish this, Tcl provides the `lappend` command. The syntax is as follows:

```
lappend variable value1 value2 …
```

How to do it…

In the following example, we will append elements to a list. Return values from the commands are provided for clarity. Enter the following command:

```
% set input {John Mary Bill}
John Mary Bill

% lappend input Tom
John Mary Bill Tom
```

How it works…

The `lappend` command has treated the variable name provided in variable as a list and appended all the following values to variable as list elements.

Assigning list elements to variables

At this point, we have created, concatenated, joined and appended to our list. Next we need to know how to assign the elements of a list to variables to be able to access the individual elements. To accomplish this, Tcl provides the `lassign` command. The syntax is as follows:

```
lassign list variable1 variable2 …
```

How to do it…

In the following example, we will assign the elements of our list to a set of variables and print out the values contained within the variables. Return values from the commands are provided for clarity. Enter the following command:

```
% lassign {John Mary Bill Tom Fred} 1 2 3
Tom Fred
% puts "$1 $2 $3"
John Mary Bill
```

How it works...

The `lassign` command accepts a list as the first argument and assigns the elements to the variables given in the following arguments. If there are more variables than list elements, they will contain empty strings. If there are more elements than variables, a list of unassigned elements will be returned, as in the preceding example with `Tom` and `Fred`. Note that the command provides no return unless the number of elements exceeds the count of the variables provided.

Retrieving an element from a list

While the ability to assign the elements of a list to variables is a wonderful method of retrieving the values, it would be beneficial to access the elements directly without the necessity of variable assignment. To accomplish this, Tcl provides the `lindex` command. The syntax is as follows:

```
lindex list index1 index2 …
```

How to do it...

In the following example, we will create a list and pass an index to the `lindex` command to retrieve the value stored at the index. Return values from the commands are provided for clarity. Enter the following command:

```
% set input {John Mary Bill}
John Mary Bill

% lindex $input 1
Mary
```

How it works...

The `lindex` command accepts the `list` parameter and treats it as a Tcl list. If the index values are provided, it will return the element referenced by the indices. Please note that a list is returned if an element is a list and that additional index values will return the elements from sublists.

Inserting elements into a list

Now that we have an introduction to the usage of indices within a list, it is time to investigate how to insert items into a list at an arbitrary position as opposed to simply appending data. To accomplish this, Tcl provides the `linsert` command. The syntax is as follows:

```
linsert list index element1 element2 …
```

How to do it…

In the following example, we will insert an element into a list at a predefined location. Return values from the commands are provided for clarity. Enter the following command:

```
% set input {John Mary Bill}
John Mary Bill
% set newinput [linsert $input 1 Tom]
John Tom Mary Bill
% puts $input
John Mary Bill
% puts $newinput
John Tom Mary Bill
```

How it works…

The `linsert` command returns a new list from the list provided by inserting additional elements just before the element referenced by the index. This was illustrated by creation of the list `newinput` and the subsequent `puts` commands to display the contents of both the original and new lists. If the value contained in the index is less than or equal to 0, it will be inserted at the beginning.

Determining the number of elements

To provide more flexibility to our programs, it will be necessary to create and maintain your lists dynamically. As this will result in a list of indeterminate size, we need a means to determine the number of elements in a list. To accomplish this, Tcl provides the `llength` command. The syntax is as follows:

```
llength list
```

How to do it...

In the following example, we will pass a list to the `llength` command to determine the number of elements the list contains. Return values from the commands are provided for clarity. Enter the following command:

```
% llength {John Mary { Bill Tom }}
3
```

How it works...

The `llength` command accepts a list (in this case, a list containing an embedded list with multiple elements) as an argument and returns a decimal string containing the number of elements. As the embedded list is a single item, in the parent list the total is `3`.

Getting a list element

As we can now determine the number of elements contained within a list, it is time to retrieve one or more of those elements. To accomplish this, Tcl provides the `lrange` command. The syntax is as follows:

```
lrange list first last
```

How to do it...

In the following example, we will pass a list to the `lrange` command to retrieve the elements contained with the indices provided. Return values from the commands are provided for clarity. Enter the following command:

```
% lrange {John Mary Bill Fred Tom Sally} 0 1
John Mary
```

How it works...

The `lrange` command accepts a valid Tcl list and returns a new list consisting of the elements referenced in the index values provided in `first` and `last` last inclusive. If the index contained in `first` is less than 0, it is treated as 0. If the index contained in `last` is greater than or equal to the number of elements, it is treated as if it were `end`, as described previously, where indexes are concerned.

Repeating elements

At some point, you may want to populate a list with a number of repeated elements. This may be for testing or various other reasons. To accomplish this, Tcl provides the `lrepeat` command. The syntax is as follows:

```
lrepeat number element1 element2 …
```

How to do it…

In the following example, we will use the `lrepeat` command to create a list of repeated characters. Return values from the commands are provided for clarity. Enter the following command:

```
% lrepeat 3 a
a a a
```

How it works…

The `lrepeat` command creates a list of the size referenced in the number variable multiplied by the number of elements.

There's more…

In the following example we will combine `lrepeat` commands to create multiple lists containing repeated characters. Return values from the commands are provided for clarity. Enter the following command:

```
% lrepeat 3 [lrepeat 3 0]
{0 0 0} {0 0 0} {0 0 0}
```

As you can see, by combining the `lrepeat` command we have created a list containing the same element repeated three times.

Replacing elements

To truly have a dynamic list we need the ability to replace existing elements with new values. To accomplish this, Tcl provides the `lreplace` command. The syntax is as follows:

```
lreplace list first last element1 element2 …
```

How to do it...

In the following example, we will use the `lreplace` command replace elements contained within a list. Return values from the commands are provided for clarity. Enter the following command:

```
% lreplace {a b c d e} 1 1 X
a X c d e
```

How it works...

The `lreplace` command returns a newly created list formed by replacing one or more elements with the values contained within the element arguments. `first` and `last` refer to the indices specifying the `first` and `last` elements to be replaced. If the list is empty, the indices are ignored.

Reversing elements

Again, to maintain the dynamics of a list, it may be necessary to reverse the elements. To accomplish this, Tcl provides the `lreverse` command. The syntax is as follows:

```
lreverse list
```

How to do it...

In the following example, we will use the `lreverse` command to reverse the elements in our list. Return values from the commands are provided for clarity. Enter the following command:

```
% lreverse {a b c d e}
e d c b a
```

How it works...

The `lreverse` command accepts a list and returns a list containing the elements in reverse order.

Searching a list

As with any data contained within a program, it is the ability to locate and use that data that makes the program usable. To accomplish this, Tcl provides not only a command, but also a full complement of option flags to tailor the search. The `lsearch` command allows us to search a list to determine if it contains a particular element. Before we explore the syntax, we will first need to understand the options. The options are as follows:

Type of option	Option name	Interpretation
Matching style options	`-exact`	The pattern is a literal string that is compared against each element.
	`-glob`	The pattern is a glob-style pattern that is matched against each element in the same manner, as a string match.
	`-regexp`	The pattern is treated as a regular expression and matched against each element.
	`-sorted`	The list elements are sorted in order. If specified, `lsearch` will use a more efficient search algorithm. The list is assumed to be sorted in ascending order and to contain ASCII strings. This option is mutually exclusive with `-glob` and `-regexp` options and is treated the same as the `-exact` option when either `-a` or `-not` is specified.
General modifier options	`-all`	The option changes the result to be a list of all matching indices (or values, if `-inline` is specified). If indices are returned, they will be in numeric order. If values are returned, the order will be that of the input list.
	`-inline`	The matching value is returned rather than the index (or an empty string, if no match exists). If the `-all` option is specified, the result will be a list of all the values that matched.
	`-not`	This option will negate the matching, returning the index of the first non-matching value.

Type of option	Option name	Interpretation
	`-start index`	The search is started at the index specified.
Content description options	`-ascii`	The list items are to be treated as Unicode strings.
	`-dictionary`	The list elements are to be compared using dictionary style comparisons (see the next chapter for more information on dictionaries).
	`-integer`	The list elements are to be compared as integers.
	`-nocase`	The comparison will be case-insensitive. This has no effect when combined with `-dictionary`, `-integer`, or `-real` options.
	`-real`	The list elements are to be compared as floating-point values.
Sorted list options	`-decreasing`	The list elements are sorted in decreasing order. This option must be used in concert with the `-sorted` option.
	`-increasing`	The list elements are to be sorted in increasing order. This option must be used in concert with the -sorted option.
Nested list options	`-index IndexList`	This option is to be used when searching within nested lists. The `IndexList` argument gives a path of indices within each element.
	`-subindices`	If this option is used, the index results from the command will be a given path within the list to the term located.

The syntax for the `lsearch` command is as follows:

```
lsearch options list pattern
```

How to do it...

In the following example, we will use the `lsearch` command to locate a specific pattern contained within a list. Return values from the commands are provided for clarity. Enter the following command:

```
% lsearch -all {John Mary Bill John Mary Bill} Bill
2 5
```

How it works...

The `lsearch` command accepts a list of arguments and based on the options specified conducts a search of the list for the pattern specified. Return values are normally the indices of the element unless the value is returned based on the options provided. Additional options, as described in the table, can be used to tailor the search and the resulting returns, as required.

Editing a list

Another method of editing the contents of a Tcl list is the `lset` command. The syntax is as follows:

```
lset variable index1 index 2 … value
```

How to do it...

In the following example, we will use the `lset` command to edit the contents of our list. Return values from the commands are provided for clarity. Enter the following command:

```
% set input {John Mary Fred}
John Mary Fred

% lset input 1 Tom
John Tom Fred
```

How it works...

The `lset` command accepts a variable containing a Tcl list and 0 or more indices. The indices may be entered singly or provided as a Tcl list. The value is the new value to place into the list in whole or in part if indices are provided.

Sorting a list

In order to sort a list Tcl has provided the `lsort` command. As with other commands this one accepts numerous options that we will cover prior to discussing the syntax. The options are as follows:

Options	Interpretations
`-ascii`	Sorts using string comparison with Unicode code-point collation order.
`-dictionary`	Sorts using dictionary style comparison.
`-integer`	Converts the list elements to integers and use integer comparison.
`-real`	Converts the list elements to floating-point values and use floating-point comparison.
`-command command`	Uses the command provided as a comparison command.
`-increasing`	Sorts in increasing order.
`-decreasing`	Sorts in decreasing order.
`-indices`	Returns a list of indices in sorted order as opposed to the values.
`-index IndexList`	For this option to be specified each element of the list must be a proper Tcl sublist.
`-nocase`	Sorts using a case-insensitive comparison.
`-unique`	Returns only the last set of duplicate items.

The syntax for the `lsort` command is as follows:

```
lsort options list
```

How to do it...

In the following example, we will use the `lsort command` to sort the contents of a list in a decreasing order. Return values from the commands are provided for clarity. Enter the following command:

```
% lsort -decreasing {a b c d e}
e d c b a
```

How it works...

Based on the options specified, the `lsort` command will return a sorted list or a sorted index if `-indices` were specified.

Splitting a string into a list

The last thing we will be covering is how to take a string and split its content into a proper Tcl list. To accomplish this, Tcl provides the `split` command. The syntax is as follows:

```
split string characters
```

How to do it…

In the following example, we will use the `split command` to separate the contents of a comma-delimited string into a list. Return values from the commands are provided for clarity. Enter the following command:

```
% split {John,Mary,Tom,Fred,Sally},
John Mary Fred Tom Sally
```

How it works…

The `split` command accepts a string and splits it into a Tcl list by splitting at every character defined. Caution must be exercised about the characters provided for splitting to avoid loss of data.

6
The Tcl Dictionary

In this chapter, we will cover the following topics:

- Creating a dictionary
- Appending to a dictionary
- Determining if a key exists
- Filtering a dictionary
- Searching a dictionary
- Getting a record
- Incrementing a value
- Getting the dictionary structure
- Getting a list of keys
- Appending to an existing record
- Merging two dictionaries
- Create a blank dictionary structure
- Updating variables from a dictionary
- Determining the size of a dictionary
- Getting all records
- Assigning values

Introduction

Strings hold textual data from a single character to a large text file. Lists allow us to store groups of strings and lists in an organized manner. But neither offers a simple method for relating data elements to a key value, in the manner of an array or database. If you need to organize multiple items under a single group, nothing beats a dictionary.

Dictionary allows storage of data with a key/value mapping methodology, with each key in the dictionary mapping to a single value. Dictionaries are textual in nature (like how lists are), but allow association between key/value pairs. For example, if I create a dictionary "Fruits" with a key of "Apple" and a value of "17"; I have the beginnings of a simple inventory system. With the addition of nested dictionaries, you can rapidly emulate data storage and retrieval similar to a database application without the overhead of a third-party product.

As with all things in Tcl, we have been provided with a command and a full complement of options to create and manage our dictionaries. In the following sections, we will cover both, the `dict` command as well as its options. The `dict` command is the workhorse for all of your dictionary needs. By pairing it with the optional keywords, you instruct the interpreter how to utilize the command. The syntax is as follows:

```
dict option argument1 argument2…
```

The `dict` command performs a function based on the option defined. Argument number and type are predicated by the option that is selected. As a pre-requisite for the recipes in this chapter, launch the Tcl shell, as appropriate for your operating system. You can access Tcl from the command line to execute the commands.

Creating a dictionary

To create a dictionary, we will utilize the `create` option. The syntax is as follows:

```
dict create key value… key value… key value…
```

How to do it...

In the following example, we will create a dictionary containing a key/value pair. Return values from the commands are provided for clarity. Enter the following command:

```
% dict create 1 John
1 John
```

How it works...

The `dict create` command creates a new dictionary that contains each of the key and value mappings that follow.

There's more...

By adding additional key/value pairs on the command line, you can store numerous entries simultaneously. In the following example, we will expand our dictionary by storing multiple key/value pairs. Return values from the commands are provided for clarity. Enter the following command:

```
% dict create 1 John 2 Mary 3 Paul
1 John 2 Mary 3 Paul
```

As you can see, the `dict create` command accepted the arguments and created a dictionary containing our three key/value pairs. Care should be taken that the key names are not inadvertently repeated, as the last instance will be the one stored. For example, if I pass in `1 John 2 Mary 1 Paul`, the value assigned to key `1` will be `Paul` and *not* `John`.

Using set with the dict create command

While the `dict create` command allows us to create a dictionary and easily add the key/value pairs, we have no named variable to allow us to access our dictionary. To allow us to access the dictionary, we will need to combine the Tcl `set` command with the `dict create` command to have a named dictionary that we can access.

In the following example, we will create a named dictionary containing multiple key/value pairs. The return values from the commands are provided for clarity. Enter the following command:

```
% set names [dict create 1 John 2 Mary 3 Paul]
1 John 2 Mary 3 Paul
```

While there is no noticeable difference in the return line, we now have a named dictionary that can be referenced by other commands. At this point, we can create a named dictionary and assign key/value pairs from the command line. However, without the ability to dynamically maintain our dictionary, it is of little use in a real-time program.

In the following sections, we will investigate the various Tcl commands that allow us to fully utilize the Tcl dictionary.

Appending to a dictionary

One way of adding key/value pairs to a dictionary is the `dict append` command. The syntax is as follows:

```
dict append name key value…
```

How to do it…

In the following example, we will create a dictionary containing a set of key/value pairs and then append an additional set. Return values from the commands are provided for clarity. Enter the following command:

```
% set names [dict create 1 John 2 Mary 3 Paul]
1 John 2 Mary 3 Paul
```

```
% dict append names 4 Fred
1 John 2 Mary 3 Paul 4 Fred
```

How it works...

The `dict append` command appends a `key and value` pair (or pairs) to the dictionary referenced by `name`.

Determining if a key exists

Now that we have a named dictionary with key/value pairs, it becomes necessary to determine if the given key exists. To accomplish this, Tcl provides the `dict exists` command. The syntax is as follows:

```
dict exists DictionaryValue key… key…
```

How to do it...

In the following example, we will create a dictionary containing a set of key/value pairs and then determine whether or not a specific key exists. Return values from the commands are provided for clarity. Enter the following command:

```
% set names [dict create 1 John 2 Mary 3 Paul]
1 John 2 Mary 3 Paul

% dict exists $names 3
1
```

How it works...

The `dict exists` command returns a Boolean value to indicate if the specified key exists in the dictionary referenced in name. A return value of `1` indicates that the key exists, while a return of `0` indicates that it does not. Be aware that this command will return an error if `dictionaryValue` does not reference an existing dictionary.

Filtering a dictionary

Filtering a dictionary in Tcl allows us to create a new dictionary containing the filtered key/value pairs, as opposed to simply returning a filtered listing. This allows us to isolate the data desired and interact with it dynamically. To accomplish this, Tcl provides the `dict filter` command. The syntax is as follows:

```
dict filter dictionaryValue filter_type argument1 argument2 …
```

Various filter types are supported by the command. The filters are as follows:

Option	Interpretation
Key	The key rule matches the key/value pair whose keys match the defined pattern, as in a string match.
Value	The value rule matches the key/value pairs whose value matches the defined pattern, as in a string match.
Script	The script rule tests for matching by assigning the key to a key variable and the value to a value variable, and then evaluating the given script, which must return a Boolean value. Only those sets that return the value `true` are included within the new dictionary. If the script returns a `TCL_BREAK`, no other comparisons are performed. In the event of a `TCL_CONTINUE` return, the return is treated as a `TCL_OK`.

How to do it…

In the following example we will create a dictionary containing a set of key/value pairs and then filter to determine if a specific key exists. Return values from the commands are provided for clarity. Enter the following command:

```
% set names [dict create 1 John 2 Mary 3 Paul]
1 John 2 Mary 3 Paul

% set filtered [dict filter $names key 1]
1 John
```

How it works…

The `dict filter` command accepts a named dictionary as referenced by `dictionaryValue` and returns a new dictionary containing the key/value pairs that match the filtering criteria as defined in the argument or arguments provided.

There's more…

In the following example, we will create a dictionary containing a set of key/value pairs and then filter to determine if a specific value exists. Return values from the commands are provided for clarity. Enter the following command:

```
% set names [dict create 1 John 2 Joe 3 Paul]
1 John 2 Joe 3 Paul
```

```
% set filtered [dict filter $names value Jo*]
1 John 2 Joe
```

As you can see, the `dict filter` command accepted the arguments and based on the existence of the value to be filtered, it has returned a new dictionary named `filtered`, containing the located key/value pairs.

In the following example, we will create a dictionary containing a set of key/value pairs and then filter to determine if a specific value exists, by using the `script` keyword. Return values from the commands are provided for clarity. Enter the following command:

```
 % set filtered [dict filter $name script {key value} {
  Expr {$key < 2}
}]
1 John
```

In this instance, the `filter` command has evaluated each key/value pair and returned those that evaluate as `true`, in the provided script.

Searching a dictionary

To iterate over a dictionary, Tcl provides the `dict for` command. The syntax is as follows:

```
dict for {key value} dictionaryValue script
```

How to do it...

In the following example, we will create a dictionary containing a set of key/value pairs and then using the dict for command return a listing of all key/value pairs using the `puts` command. Return values from the commands are provided for clarity. Enter the following command:

```
% set names [dict create 1 John 2 Mary 3 Paul]
1 John 2 Mary 3 Paul

% dict for {id data} $names {
puts "Key $id : Value $data"
}
Key 1 : Value John
Key 2 : Value Mary
Key 3 : Value Paul
```

How it works...

The `dict for` command accepts three arguments. The first argument is a two-element list of variable names for the `key` and `value`. The second is the dictionary that is to be searched. The third is a script to be evaluated for each mapping with the key and variable values set, as in the `foreach` command.

Getting a record

While the `dict for` command is generally used for processing multiple key/value pairs, Tcl provides the `dict get` command to obtain the value assigned to a specific key. The syntax is as follows:

```
dict get dictionaryValue key
```

How to do it...

In the following example, we will create a dictionary containing a set of key/value pairs and then, using the `dict get` command, obtain the value associated with the specified key. Return values from the commands are provided for clarity. Enter the following command:

```
% set names [dict create 1 John 2 Mary 3 Paul]
1 John 2 Mary 3 Paul

% dict get $names 3
Paul
```

How it works...

The `dict get` command will retrieve the value associated with the argument contained in the `key` for the dictionary defined by `dictionaryValue`.

Incrementing a value

Tcl provides a simple method for incrementing a value stored within a dictionary with the `dict incr` command. This is extremely useful when storing numeric values in the dictionary. The syntax is as follows:

```
dict incr dictionaryValue key increment
```

How to do it...

In the following example, we will create a dictionary containing a key/value pair and then using the `dict incr` command, we will increase the value associated with the key specified. Return values from the commands are provided for clarity. Enter the following command:

```
% set numbers [dict create one 1]
one 1
% dict incr $numbers one 3
one 4
```

How it works...

The `dict incr` command will increase the value stored in `key` by the amount defined within the increment parenthesis for the dictionary referenced by `dictionaryValue`.

Getting the dictionary structure

In order to assist us with managing our dictionaries Tcl provides the `dict info` command. The syntax is as follows:

```
dict info dictionaryValue
```

How to do it...

In the following example we will create a dictionary containing a key/value pair and then using the `dict info` command obtain information for our dictionary. Return values from the commands are provided for clarity. Enter the following command:

```
% set names [dict create 1 John 2 Mary 3 Paul]
1 John 2 Mary 3 Paul
% dict info $names
3 entries in table, 4 buckets
number of buckets with 0 entries: 1
number of buckets with 1 entries: 3
number of buckets with 2 entries: 0
number of buckets with 3 entries: 0
number of buckets with 4 entries: 0
number of buckets with 5 entries: 0
number of buckets with 6 entries: 0
```

```
number of buckets with 7 entries: 0
number of buckets with 8 entries: 0
number of buckets with 9 entries: 0
number of buckets with 10 or more entries: 0
average search distance for entry: 1.0
```

How it works...

The `dict info` command returns human readable information about the dictionary referenced in `dictionaryValue`.

Getting a list of keys

In order to minimize effort on dictionary maintenance Tcl has provided the `dict keys` command to return a list of keys that exist within a dictionary. The syntax is as follows:

```
dict keys dictionaryValue pattern
```

How to do it...

In the following example we will create a dictionary containing a collection of key/value pairs and then using the `dict keys` command obtain a list of valid keys. Return values from the commands are provided for clarity. Enter the following command:

```
% set test [dict create 1 John 2 Mary 3 Paul]
1 John 2 Mary 3 Paul

% dict keys $test
1 2 3
```

How it works...

The `dict keys` command returns a list of keys that exists within the dictionary referenced by `dictionaryValue`. If a pattern is supplied, only those keys that match are returned.

Appending to an existing record

To append data to an existing value Tcl provides the `dict lappend` command. The syntax is as follows:

```
dict lappend name key value…
```

How to do it…

In the following example, we will create a dictionary containing a collection of key/value pairs and then using the `dict lappend` command we will append items to the key referenced. Return values from the commands are provided for clarity. Enter the following command:

```
% set test [dict create 1 1 2 2 3 3]

1 1 2 2 3 3

% dict lappend test 2 more
1 1 2 {2 more} 3 3
```

How it works…

The `dict lappend` command appends the data stored in `value` for the key referenced in `key` for the dictionary specified in `name`.

Merging two dictionaries

Let's assume that we have two dictionaries that we need to merge into a single dictionary. To accomplish this, Tcl provides the `dict merge` command. The syntax is as follows:

```
dict merge dictionaryValue1 dictionaryValue2…
```

How to do it…

In the following example, we will create two dictionaries containing collections of key/value pairs and then using the `dict merge` command create a dictionary containing the contents of both. Return values from the commands are provided for clarity. Enter the following command:

```
% set test1 [dict create 1 John 2 Mary 3 Paul]
1 John 2 Mary 3 Paul

% set test2 [dict create 4 Fred 5 Sue 6 Tom]
4 Fred 5 Sue 6 Tom
```

```
% set merged [dict merge $test1 $test2]
1 John 2 Mary 3 Paul 4 Fred 5 Sue 6 Tom
```

How it works...

The `dict merge` command returns a dictionary containing the contents of two or more dictionaries, as specified in the `dictionaryValue` arguments. In the event of duplicate key mapping, the last dictionary merged will be the value that will be used. For example, if there are two dictionaries that contain a key with different values, the second dictionary key/value mapping would be retained.

Creating a blank dictionary structure

To create a new dictionary structure that contains some or all of the key/value mappings present in an existing dictionary, Tcl provides the `dict remove` command. The syntax is as follows:

```
dict remove dictionayValue key1… key2…
```

How to do it...

In the following example we will create a dictionary containing collections of key/value pairs and then using the `dict remove` command create a new dictionary containing a portion of the key/value pairs. Return values from the commands are provided for clarity. Enter the following command:

```
% set test [dict create 1 John 2 Mary 3 Paul]
1 John 2 Mary 3 Paul

% set new [dict remove $test 2]
1 John 3 Paul
```

How it works...

As you can see, the `dict remove` command has created a new dictionary that contains only the desired key/value pairs. In our example, the key/value pair for key `2` was removed.

Updating variables from a dictionary

To update the values stored within a dictionary Tcl provides the `dict set` command. The syntax of this command is as follows:

```
dict set name key value… key value…
```

How to do it…

In the following example, we will create a dictionary containing collections of key/value pairs and then using the `dict set` we will update a stored value. Return values from the commands are provided for clarity. Enter the following command:

```
% set test [dict create 1 John 2 Mary 3 Paul]
1 John 2 Mary 3 Paul

% dict set test 2 Martha
1 John 2 Martha 3 Paul
```

How it works…

The `dict set` command updates the value stored for the `key` in the dictionary referenced to by the `name` argument.

Determining the size of a dictionary

To more effectively interact with a dictionary, it is beneficial to know how many entries are contained within. To accomplish this, Tcl provides the `dict size` command. The syntax is as follows:

```
dict size dictionaryValue
```

How to do it…

In the following example, we will create a dictionary containing collections of key/value pairs and then we will use the `dict size` command to determine the number of key/value pairs. Return values from the commands are provided for clarity. Enter the following command:

```
% set test [dict create 1 John 2 Mary 3 Paul]
1 John 2 Mary 3 Paul

% dict size $test
3
```

How it works...

The `dict size` command returns a count of the key/value pairs contained in the dictionary.

Getting all records

Whereas the `dict keys` command returns a listing of all keys contained within a dictionary, the `dict values` command will return a listing of all stored values. The syntax is as follows:

```
dict values dictionaryValue
```

How to do it...

In the following example we will create a dictionary containing collections of key/value pairs and then using the `dict values` command we will obtain a list of all values stored within the dictionary. Return values from the commands are provided for clarity. Enter the following command:

```
% set test [dict create 1 one 2 two 3 three]
1 one 2 two 3 three

% dict values $test
one two three
```

How it works...

The `dict values` command will return a list of all values stored within the dictionary specified in `dictionaryValue`.

Assigning values

In this section we will be creating a nested dictionary containing multiple entries for each record. By using the Tcl `dict with` command we will then assign variables in the body of our script that are based on the keys stored within our dictionary. The `dict with` command allows us to accomplish this by assigning entries within our dictionary to variables and then executing a script. The syntax is as follows:

```
dict with name keys… script
```

How to do it...

In the following example, we will create a nested dictionary to hold a collection of key/value pairs and then using the `dict for` and `with` commands we will execute a script to output the values to the screen. Return values from the commands are provided for clarity. Enter the following command:

```
% set person1 [dict create firstname John lastname Smith title Manager]
firstname John lastname Smith title Manager

% set person2 [dict create firstname Mary lastname Jones title Developer]
firstname Mary lastname Jones title Developer}

% set record [dict create 12345 $person1 12346 $person2]
12345 {firstname John lastname Smith title Manager} 12346 {firstname Mary
lastname Jones title Developer}

% dict for {id info} $record {
puts "Record #: $id"
dict with info {
puts "Title: $title"
puts "Name: $lastname, $firstname"
}
}
Record #: 12345
Title: Manager
Name: Smith, John
Record #: 12346
Title: Developer
Name: Jones, Mary
```

7
File Operations

In this chapter, we will cover:

- Opening a file
- Configuring a file
- Opening a command pipeline
- Writing a file
- Reading a file
- Closing a file
- File handling

Introduction

Up to this point, we have primarily entered the data through the command line. While this is fine for small scripts, it does not provide the means to obtain and store information. To accomplish this, we need to read and write to the file system.

File access is a basic requirement for dynamic programs. Whether it's a text-based configuration file or images to display, most programs use the file system as the storage and retrieval location. All storage needs have—historically and continually—relied on the file system.

Although we will be dealing with strings in the coming sections, the requirements for accessing any type of file, from the string data to images, remain the same.

In the following sections, for the majority of the examples, we will be accessing the file system to read and write the data to a file. To accomplish this, you will need to launch your Tcl shell appropriately, based on your operating platform and follow the instructions.

Opening a file

The first item we will cover is how to open a file. When you open a file, Tcl creates what it refers to as a "channel" that can be read from and written to. Channels are also created for serial ports, external command pipelines, and when opening sockets.

The Tcl command to open a file is aptly named `open`. The `open` command accepts numerous flags to control access and permissions. These are covered in the following:

Access	Interpretation
r	Opens the file for reading only.
	The file must already exist.
	Default access.
r+	Opens the file for reading and writing.
	The file must already exist.
w	Opens the file for writing only.
	The file *will* be truncated if it already exists.
	If no named file exists, it will be created.
w+	Opens the file for reading and writing.
	The file *will* be truncated if it already exists.
	If the named file does not exist, it will be created.
a	Opens the file for writing only.
	If the named file does not exist, it will be created.
	This will set the file pointer (to the point at which writing will commence) to the end of the file prior to each write.
a+	Opens the file for reading and writing.
	If the named file does not exist, it will be created.
	Sets the file pointer to the end of the file.

All the legal access in the table may have the character '`b`' added as the second or third character (for example `wb`) to indicate that the open channel should be configured for binary access. Additionally, the file access can be altered after it has been opened with the `fconfigure` command covered in the next section.

In the second acceptable form, access consists of a list of the following flags, all of which have the standard POSIX meaning. One of the flags *must* be `RDONLY`, `WRONLY`, or `RDWR`.

Permission	Interpretation
RDONLY	Opens the file for read only.
WRONLY	Opens the file for writing only.
RDWR	Opens the files for read and write access.
APPEND	Sets the file pointer to the end of the file prior to each write.
BINARY	Configures the channel for binary access.
CREAT	Creates the file if it does not exist.
EXCL	If CREAT is also specified, an error is returned if the file exists.
NOCTTY	If the file is a terminal device, this will prevent the file from controlling terminal processes.
NONBLOCK	Prevents the process from blocking while opening the file. The behavior of this flag is system and device dependant.
TRUNC	If the file exists, it *will* be truncated.

If a new file is created as part of the opening, permissions (as an integer) are used to set the permissions for the new file in conjunction with the processes' file mode creation. Permissions, by default, provide full access.

Now that we have covered the access types and setting of permissions, let's look at the syntax of the command. The syntax is as follows:

```
open filename access permissions
```

How to do it...

Enter the following command:

```
% set fp [open text.txt a+]
file5
```

How it works...

As you can see the `open` command has returned a file pointer named `file5` to our existing file with the permissions set to `a+`. See the preceding tables for an explanation of the permission notations. Please note that the file pointer is intended to be an opaque value and may not be the same for subsequent invocations.

The `open` command will open the file referenced by `filename` with the `access` type and `permissions` provided and return a file pointer. Note that we have paired this with the `set` command to allow access to the file pointer named `fp`. This is the standard method, as access to the pointer is required to interact with the file.

Bear it in mind that the access types may have hazardous consequences, if utilized improperly. For example, opening a configuration file with the access set to `w` will result in the file being truncated. This is probably not the method you wish to use for critical data that needs to be retained.

There's more...

Now enter the following command line:

```
% set fp [open bad.txt RDONLY]
couldn't open "bad.txt": no such file or directory
```

As we have attempted to access a non-existent file, the Tcl error text for the command was displayed.

Configuring a file

As mentioned previously, you may use the `fconfigure` command to set or get the configuration options for an open channel. The syntax is as follows:

```
fconfigure channel name value name value...
```

If invoked with no option names or values, the `fconfigure` command will return the configuration options for the channel specified. Optionally, a configuration name may be passed to get the configurations for the option specified. If name and value pairs are passed the file will be configured based on the name/value pairs supplied.

The syntax of acceptable options and their descriptions are as follows:

Option	Description
`-blocking boolean`	This determines if the I/O operations can result in indefinite blocking. Acceptable values must be provided in the standard Tcl Boolean format.
`-buffering value`	If set to `full` all output is buffered until a `flush` command is invoked. If set to `line`, then the system will automatically flush when a newline character is output. If set to `none` the system will flush after each operation.
`-buffersize size`	The value of `size` may be any valid integer value. This will configure the size for the buffer s in bytes and allocate the specified amount for the channel.
`-encoding name`	This will set the encoding for the channel to allow data to be converted to and from Unicode for use by Tcl. Default encoding is system and locale specific.

Option	Description
`-eofchar char`	Specifies the end of file character.
`-translation mode`	Acceptable values for mode are as follows: `auto` treats any newline, carriage return or carriage return/ newline as the end of line representation. `binary` no end of line translations are performed. `cr` specifies that the end of line character is a carriage return. `crlf` specifies that the end of line character is a carriage return/ linefeed pair. `Lf` specifies that the end of line character is a linefeed.

How to do it...

Enter the following command:

```
% set fp [open text.txt r]
file3f40


$fconfigure $fp
-blocking 1 -buffering full -buffersize 4096 -encoding cp1252 -eofchar ->
\
 -translation auto
```

In the preceding example, we have returned the current options for the file specified by `$fp`. To obtain a single value, we would perform the following:

```
% fconfigure $fp -buffersize
4096
```

There's more...

Now enter the following command line:

```
% fconfigure $fp -blocking 0
% fconfigure $fp -blocking
 0
```

In the first command, we have set the blocking for `$fp` to `false` by passing a `0`. The second line returned the value for blocking, based on the new configuration.

Opening a command pipeline

As mentioned previously, the open command can be used to open a command pipeline. A **command pipeline** is a mechanism that allows us to read from or write to a command. The syntax is similar to the standard open command. However, if the first character passed as an argument to the open command is a pipe character (|) the remaining characters are treated as a list of arguments describing a command pipeline that is to be invoked. The syntax is as follows:

```
open | command access_permissions
```

The arguments provided by command are similar to those used for the exec command. The open command will return a file pointer that may be used to write to the specified command's input pipe or read from its output pipe. The specific functionality (read or write) is determined by the access permissions.

If the open command or one of the commands provided as arguments should return an error, a Tcl error will be generated when the close command is invoked on the channel unless the pipeline has been configured for non-blocking. If the channel is configured for non-blocking, no exit status will be returned.

How to do it...

Enter the following command:

```
%set fp [open "|cmd.exe /c dir text.txt" r]
fileabb5b0

%set data [read $fp]
 Volume in drive C has no label.
 Volume Serial Number is A02F-AD99

 Directoy of C:\Documents and Settings\Bert

12/09/2010 01:01 PM        13 text.txt
        1 File(s)          13 bytes
        0 Dir(s) 31,133,941,760 bytes free

%If {[catch {close $fp} err]} {
  Puts "Error: $err"
}
%
```

How it works...

As you can see, the `open` command has returned a file pointer named `fileabb5b0` to our command. Also, note that because the command was invoked on a Windows platform additional command syntax was required to access the `dir` command. This is due to the fact that Windows built-in commands are not implemented by using the executables themselves. This is not required on a Unix- or a Linux-based system.

The return of the command was accessible as we had set the file privileges to `r` (open the file for "read-only" and the file must exist) and the return was read into our `data` variable and displayed on the console. The returns are specific to your platform and will vary based on the platform and path variables in place.

We next used a `catch` statement to trap any errors that might have resulted. These would be returned by the `close` command. As we successfully executed our `dir` command, there were no error codes returned and the `catch` statement simply returned us to our console prompt without invoking the `puts` command.

There's more...

Now enter the following command line:

```
%set fp [open "|cmd.exe /c dir no_such_file" r]
fileaca748

%set data [read $fp]
 Volume in drive C has no label.
 Volume Serial Number is A02F-AD99

 Directoy of C:\Documents and Settings\Bert

%If {[catch {close $fp} err]} {
       Puts "Error: $err"
}
ERROR: File Not Found
%
```

In this instance, we have performed the same command with the exception that we have referenced a non-existing file. As you can see, the `catch` command has trapped the error return and the `puts` command was used to display it on the console. Please note that the basic return from the command was displayed when we set the variable `data` with the `read` command, but this is not always indicative of a successful return code.

Writing a file

Writing to a file is accomplished in the same manner as writing to the console. Using the `puts` command with the addition of a file channel descriptor will result in the string provided being written to the channel. The syntax is as follows:

```
puts -nonewline channel string
```

How to do it...

Enter the following command:

```
% set fp [open text.txt a]
file5
% puts $fp "Hello Again"
% flush $fp
```

How it works...

The `puts` command will write the data contained in `string` to the referenced `file pointer`. If the optional `-nonewline` switch is provided the newline character will not be added. Bear in mind that if you are not closing the file following the write action, it is necessary to `flush` the channel to complete the write. The channel is automatically flushed when the file pointer is closed or when the application exits.

To check the file, open it with the text editor of your choice. You should see a file that contains the following:

```
Hello World
```

Reading a file

Reading a file allows us to retrieve the stored data from the open channel. To accomplish this Tcl provides the `read` command. The command utilizes two forms. The syntax is as follows:

```
read -nonewline channel
read channel number
```

How to do it...

Enter the following command:

```
% set fp [open text.txt r]
file5
% read $fp
Hello World
```

How it works...

In the first form, the `read` command reads *all* the data from the `channel`. If the optional `-nonewline` switch is provided then the last character of the file is discarded if it is a newline. In the second form, the `number` argument instructs the command to return the number of characters specified unless there are fewer characters in the file in which case all characters will be returned.

By using the `read` command we accessed the channel and the data read from the file was displayed. As referenced in the previous tables detailing access permissions, the channel can be set to non-blocking with the optional `NONBLOCK` POSIX keyword. If the channel is configured for non-blocking, you may not obtain all data available rather than blocking for more data. This is of primary importance when dealing with open sockets, serial ports, and command channels.

Optionally, you may read from a file by utilizing the `gets` command. This command reads the file line by line and is invoked with the following syntax:

```
gets channel optionalVariable
```

This command will read in the next line from the channel referenced by `channel` and display it to the screen if no `optionalVariable` is provided. If an `optionalVariable` is provided, it will be set to the contents of the line read in.

Closing a file

After any write to a file, you should close it to complete the process. Although exiting a program will close the channel, this is not my preferred manner as a program error may result in the loss of any data that has not been written to disk. To close the file, Tcl provides the `close` command. The syntax is as follows:

```
close channel
```

How to do it...

Enter the following command:

```
% set fp [open text.txt a]
file5
% puts $fp "Hello Again"
% close $fp
```

How it works...

The `close` command flushes the open channel of any pending data resulting in a write to disk and closes the channel. As you can see the `close` command has closed the file successfully as there were no errors returned.

To check the file, open it with your text editor of choice. You should see a file that contains the following:

```
Hello World
Hello Again
```

File handling

Now that we can open, read, write, and close a file, it is time to put this knowledge to work in a real world manner. We will now create a Tcl script that accesses a file, reorders the stored data, and then outputs it to a secondary file. This is similar to a file handling procedure used to clean up user supplied files.

Getting ready

Using the text editor of your choice create a text file containing the following text:

```
1,3,5,7,8,2,4,6,9
```

Save the file in your working directory as `input.txt`.

How to do it...

Using the text editor of your choice create the following Tcl script and save it in your working directory as `filehandler.tcl`.

```
# Check that a filename was provided
if { $argc>0 & $argv>0} {
 # Assign the filename to a variable
```

```
set fname [lindex $argv 0]
# Open the file for read-only access
set fp [open $fname r]
# Read the contents of the file into a variable
set data [read $fp]
#Close the input file
close $fp
# Split the data and create a Tcl list
set input [split $data ","]
# Sort the list and load it into another list
set output [lsort -increasing $input]
# Open a file to write the data to
set fp [open output.txt w]
# Read through the list and write the data
foreach item $output {
 puts $fp $item
}
#Close the file
close $fp
} else {
puts "No filename provided... Exiting Script"
exit
}
```

Launch your Tcl shell appropriately, based on your operating platform. Enter the following command line:

```
% tclsh filehandler.tcl input.txt
%
```

How it works...

By combining the capabilities of the Tcl, file handling commands with the Tcl list functionality we are able to read in a comma delimited list of data and output it to a file sorted and line-by-line. To confirm the output, use the text editor of your choice and view the file `output.txt`. It should contain a sorted listing of the integers provided, one per line, as shown next:

```
1
2
3
4
5
6
7
8
9
```

8
Tk GUI Programming with Tcl/Tk

In this chapter, we will cover:

- Creating a widget
- Writing to the console
- Window manager
- Creating a window
- Destroying a window
- Creating a custom dialog

Introduction

Up to this point, we have exclusively used the Tcl shell and its command set. While this is a wonderful method for writing scripts and non-graphical programs, it fails to provide the end user with a **Graphical User Interface** (**GUI**) to interact with. To allow for the creation and control of GUI and window elements, Tcl includes the **Graphical Tool Kit** (**Tk**).

Tk is a platform-independent GUI framework included in the Tcl package. By using the native Tk widgets and applying the correct theme, the GUI elements can be made to assume the native look and feel of the system on which they run, providing a polished appearance. Tk provides a full complement of window controls such as buttons, text boxes, and labels. In addition to the standard controls, Tk also includes several top-level dialog windows (for example File Selection, Color Picker, and so on) and includes three methods of geometry management. Additional third-party packages are available to provide expanded functionality and additional controls, many of which are open source. Add to this the fact that almost all features of a widget are customizable during design or runtime, and you are allowed to have a GUI framework that is capable of creating dynamic applications that provide real-time user interaction and feedback with minimal effort on the part of the developer.

As we are now venturing into the creation and manipulation of the GUI, it is more important than ever to ensure the maintainability of your programs. The best method of doing this is by writing your programs with a debugging mindset. What I mean by this is to keep in mind the future requirements to read and understand your, when you design and write your programs.

Imagine the number of commands, windows and widgets (A **widget** is a Tk control; text box, label, image, and so on) that are required for a standard data entry interface. Buttons, text boxes, menus, labels, and all the other items necessary for interacting with the end user each have a potentially large amount of coding involved. If you design and write with the requirement of returning to the program, or the requirement for another programmer to perform these actions, you can greatly simplify the maintenance of your programs.

I have found that I can address most, if not all of these concerns with a few simple actions. First consider the syntax. Tk allows you the freedom to display widgets in a very free form manner. However, by following a consistent method of widget creation you can speed up the maintenance and greatly improve the readability of your coding. While there are no set rules, try to follow a standardized methodology in how your widgets are defined.

As you include error handling in your programs keep the concept of maintainability in mind at all times. Non-descriptive or worse, humorous, error messages and logs can not only result in an unprofessional product, but create a situation where the upkeep of your program is frustrating at best and downright embarrassing in some situations. I have seen an "Oops, something went wrong!" error message on more occasions than I care to remember.

To access and control our widgets, we will need to activate the **Window Shell** (**wish**) in the same manner as the **Tcl Shell** (**tclsh**). To access the wish shell, simply enter `wish` at the command line. As soon as you enter the `wish` command, Tk will create a window on which all the widgets will be displayed as in the following image:

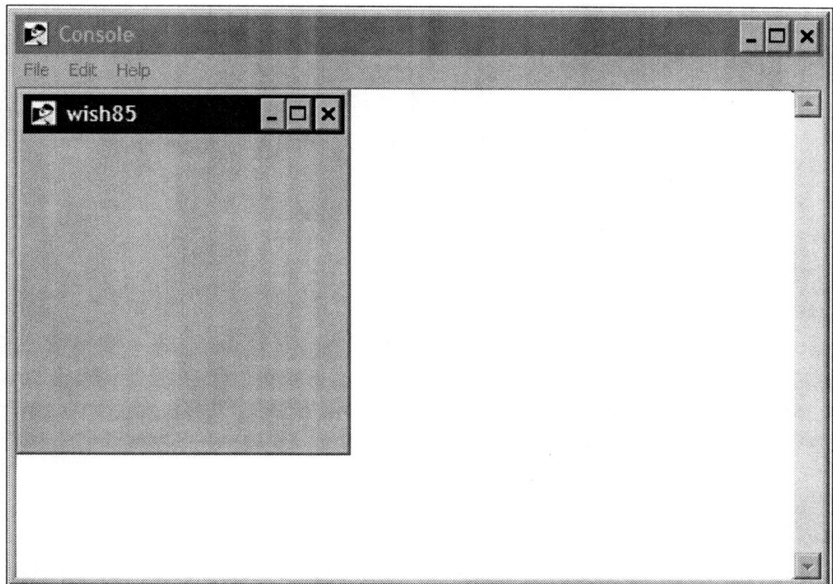

Any widget based on window commands will automatically update the window as soon as you press *Enter*, unless of course there is an error. In the event of an error, it will be displayed within the wish console. In the following sections, we will introduce widgets, writing to the wish console, and basic windowing.

To complete the following examples, we will need to access wish from the command line. Launch the wish shell appropriately for your operating system and follow the instructions provided in each section.

Creating a widget

The basic method for creating a widget is the same regardless of the widget being created. The differences are in the properties of the widget and if any action can be assigned to it. In the following chapters, we will investigate specific widgets and their properties in depth, but before we reach this point, I would like to introduce you to the button widget and some basic features.

How to do it...

In the following example, we will create a button widget with some basic properties and a single action. Enter the following commands:

```
1 % button .b -text "Exit" -command exit
2 % pack .b
```

At this point, your window should look like the following:

How it works...

The first line instructs the wish shell to create a button named `b`, which is a child of the parent window identified by the '`.`' character. This button will have a text label containing the word `Exit` and it will execute the `exit` command when clicked. Now click on the button that you have created. You will see that you have exited the wish program by activating the `exit` command.

There's more...

As I stated in the previous section, the basic method for creating a widget is the same regardless of which widget is being created. To illustrate this, we will now create a simple label containing some text. To accomplish this, enter the following commands:

```
1 % label .l -text "Label"
2 % pack .l
```

At this point, your window should look like the following:

In the button example, we created a widget by specifying the `label` widget and set its `text` property to contain the string "**Label**".

Since version 8.5, Tk has included themed widgets. They are designed to mimic the appearance of the native operating system and provide a consistent look and feel to our applications.

These widgets are accessed by invoking the `ttk::` namespace. For example, where we created our button with the `button` command, we would access the themed widgets via the `ttk::button` command, as opposed to the `button` command.

Writing to the console

Although rarely used in live programs, the console is a valuable tool during initial development. It allows us to direct debugging information easily, without requiring the overhead of creating dialog boxes (covered later in this book). To allow us to display a console on systems that have no console, or to reveal a hidden console, Tcl provides the `console` command. The `console` command accepts four keywords as follows:

Keyword	Interpretation
`eval script`	Evaluate the script argument as a Tcl script within the console interpreter.
`hide`	Hide the console.
`show`	Display the console.
`title string`	Query OR modify the console title.

The syntax is as follows:

```
console keyword argument
```

How to do it...

In the following example, we will hide the console and then create a set of buttons to display the console and to write a message. Enter the following commands:

```
% button .b -text "Show Console" -command {console show}
% button .c -text "Message" -command {puts "My Message"}
% pack .b .c
% console hide
```

At this point, your window should look like the following:

How it works...

The first line instructs the wish shell to create a button named `b`, which is a child of the parent window identified by the '`.`' character. This button will have a text label containing `Show Console` and it will execute the `console show` command when clicked. The second line instructs the wish shell to create a button named `c`, which is a child of the parent window identified by the '`.`' character. This button will have a text label containing `Message` and it will execute the `puts` command when clicked. Next, we have used the pack command (this command is a windowing geometry manager) to pack our buttons followed by hiding the console.

Now click on the `Show Console` button. At this point, the console will be visible. Next we will click on the `Message` button to display the desired text. Using this methodology you can easily direct messages to the console and provide yourself and your end user with information.

Setting the attributes of the window through window manager

The window manager is accessed from Tcl with the `wm` command. The `wm` command allows you to interact with the window manager to control the appearance and geometry of the window. The color, size, titles, and other attributes are controlled via this command. The `wm` command accepts numerous keywords. The syntax is as follows:

```
wm keyword window arguments
```

How to do it...

In the following example, we will create a window and set the title and size to be displayed. Enter the following commands:

```
1 % wm title . "My Window"
2 % wm geometry . 320x240
```

At this point, your window should look like the following:

How it works...

The `wm` command alters the appearance of the window, based on the keywords and options specified.

Creating an additional window

As you have seen simply invoking the wish shell automatically creates a window for our needs. However, many programs require the creation of secondary windows. To assist us in this process Tcl has provided the `toplevel` command. The `toplevel` command accepts several options as listed next:

Standard options:

- `-borderwidth` or `-bd`: Specifies a non-negative value indicating the width of the 3D border to draw around the outside of the window
- `-cursor`: Specifies the mouse cursor to be used for the window
- `-highlightbackground`: Specifies the color to display in the traversal highlight region when the window does not have the input focus
- `-highlightcolor`: Specifies the color to use for the traversal highlight rectangle that is drawn around the window when it has the input focus
- `-highlightthickness`: Specifies a non-negative value indicating the width of the highlight rectangle to draw around the outside of the window
- `-padx`: Specifies a non-negative value indicating how much extra space to request for the window in the X-direction
- `-pady`: Specifies a non-negative value indicating how much extra space to request for the window in the Y-direction

- `-relief`: Specifies the 3-D effect desired for the window. Acceptable values are raised, sunken, flat, ridge, solid, and groove
- `-takefocus`: Determines if the window accepts the focus during keyboard traversal

Window-specific options

- `-background`: Specifies the background color to use when drawing.
- `-class`: Specifies a class for the window.
- `-colormap`: Specifies a color map to use for the window.
- `-container`: The value must be a Boolean value. If true, it means that this window will be used as a container in which some other application will be embedded (for example, a Tk top level can be embedded using the `-use` option). The window will support the appropriate window manager protocols for things such as geometry requests. The window should not have any children of its own in this application. This option may not be changed with the configure window command.
- `-height, height, Height`: Specifies the desired height for the window.
- `-menu, menu, Menu`: Specifies a menu widget to be used as a menu bar.
- `-screen`: Specifies the screen on which the new window is placed.
- `-use, use, Use`: This option is used for embedding. If the value is not an empty string, it must be the window identifier of a container window, specified as a hexadecimal string like the ones returned by the `winfo` id command. The top level window will be created as a child of the given container instead of the root window for the screen. If the container window is in a Tk application, it must be a frame or top level window for which the `-container` option was specified. This option may not be changed with the configure window command.
- `-visual, visual, Visual`: Specifies visual information for the new window.
- `-width, width, Width`: Specifies the desired width for the window.

Commands

- `pathname cget option`: Returns the current value of the configuration option given by option.
- `pathname configure option value option value`: Query or modify the configuration options of the window.

  The syntax is as follows:

  ```
  toplevel name options
  ```

How to do it...

In the following example, we will create a window and set the title and size to be displayed while still retaining the original window. Enter the following commands:

```
1 % toplevel .top -width 320 -height 240
2 % wm title .top "My Window"
```

At this point, your top level window should be displayed in addition to the console and default window:

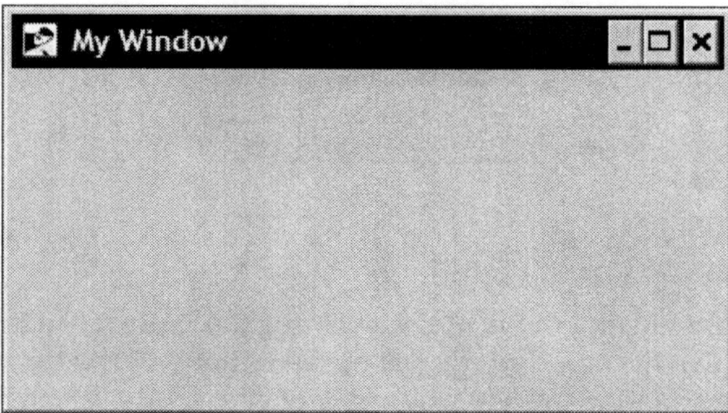

How it works...

By invoking the `toplevel` command, we have created a second window that can be configured at creation (as with the size) or by using the `wm` command, as seen in setting the title.

Destroying a window

In the first example, we configured our button widget to execute the `exit` command to close the program. Unfortunately, the `exit` command closes the wish shell as well. In order to close a window, as well as any individual widget, Tk provides the `destroy` command. The syntax is as follows:

```
destroy window
```

The `destroy` command unloads the window specified, widget or multiples thereof and in the case of the root window "." it will stop all currently running processes.

How to do it...

In the following example, we will again create a window. However, this time we will add a button widget to close our new window. Enter the following commands:

```
1 % toplevel .top
2 % button .top.b -text "Close Me" -command {destroy .top}
3 % pack .top.b
```

At this point, your window should look like the following:

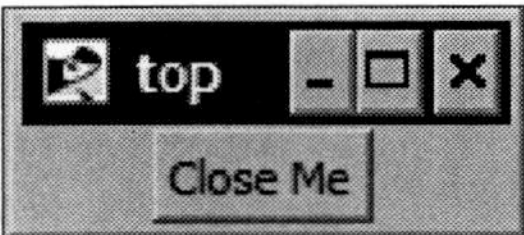

How it works...

By clicking on the button labeled **Close Me**, we will call the `destroy` command to destroy the new top level window. Do this now and you will observe that only the top level window closes while the original window and wish shell stay resident.

There's more...

In addition to the `destroy` command, Tk provides the keyword `withdraw` for the `wm` command. This keyword will cause the window specified to be withdrawn from the screen as well as to be forgotten by the window manager. The syntax is:

```
wm withdraw window
```

The `withdraw` keyword of the `wm` command will cause the `window` specified to be withdrawn from the screen and to be unmapped and forgotten by the window manager. Let's try our previous sample and replace the `destroy` command with the `withdraw` command. Enter the following commands:

```
1 % toplevel .top
2 % button .top.b -text "Close Me" -command {wm withdraw .top}
3 % pack .top.b
```

You will once again be presented with a window and button that appear identical to what we saw previously, however the underlying method of removing the window has changed. Click on the button labeled **Close Me** and you will see that the window is once again removed from view. The difference is that we have withdrawn the window as opposed to destroying it.

You may be asking yourself why you would use `wm withdraw` over `destroy` or vice versa. The reason to choose `withdraw` is that it does not `destroy` the window. The window still exists and can be redisplayed with the `wm deiconify` command. This will allow us to reuse the same window numerous times without the overhead of completely creating it again from the start. If we have no intention of accessing the window again within our program, then we would use the `destroy` command.

For example, if we need to display a window containing an error message, we can reuse the same window by simply changing the text displayed and using the `wm deiconfiy` command to return it to view. Enter the following command:

```
wm deiconify .top
```

You will now see that our window has returned to view. Clicking on the **Close Me** button will once again trigger the `wm withdraw` command.

Creating a custom dialog

Now let's pull all this together to create a custom dialog window. This is the same procedure you will use numerous times as you develop your programs. Our custom dialog will simply display a label widget and have a close button, but the basic methodology is the same that you will utilize regardless of how complex your dialog needs may be.

How to do it...

In the following example, we again will create our custom dialog window. Enter the following commands:

```
1 % toplevel .top
2 % label .top.msg -text "This is my Custom Dialog"
3 % button .top.ok -text "OK" -command {destroy .top}
4 % pack .top.ok -side bottom -fill x
5 % pack .top.msg -expand 1 -fill both
```

At this point, your window should look like the following:

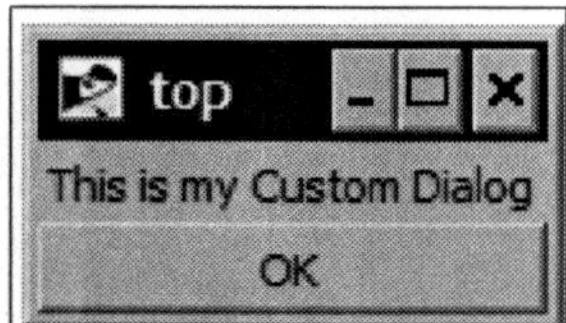

How it works...

The `toplevel` command has drawn the custom dialog window. We have added the widgets (in this case, a label, and a button) to display the information and facilitate user interaction. Click the **OK** button and once again you will remove our custom dialog window without closing the wish shell or original window. The additional parameters passed to the `pack` command control the specific placement of the widgets and will be addressed in following chapters.

9
Configuring and Controlling Tk Widgets

In this chapter, we will cover:

- Creating a frame widget
- Creating a label widget
- Creating an entry widget
- Creating a button widget
- Creating a listbox widget
- Creating an image
- Creating a simple form

Introduction

In the following sections, we will explore some of the most commonly used Tk widgets. By utilizing these widgets, you can easily create a data entry style form that includes not only input and informative screen text, but also provides user interaction with the help of button controls. In addition, the image command allows for the display of graphics to provide an interface to the graphical data, as well as creating a polished look and feel, by displaying images on the interface.

To complete the following examples, we will need to access wish from the command line. Launch the wish shell as appropriate for your operating system and follow the instructions provided in each section.

The syntax for all widgets is as follows:

```
widget path keyword value
```

Create an element of the type specified by the command referenced in widget (frame, button, and so on) with the path specified with one or more listed keyword and value pairs. Specific keywords for each widget will be listed in the individual sections.

Creating a frame widget

The **frame widget** is used as a container for other widgets. Although it works in and of itself, it accepts no input from the user nor does it provide feedback. It simplifies the layout of complex screens and adds to the appearance of the final product. To add a widget to a frame, we use the following syntax:

```
% 1 frame .f
% 2 button .f.b -text "My Button"
```

The naming hierarchy in Tcl is such that we prepend the name of the container. In this case, a frame is prepended to the button to instruct the interpreter that the button is contained within a container. A container can be a window, top level, canvas, or frame, as in the previous example.

The keywords are described in the Tk main pages as follows:

Standard keywords	Interpretation
`-borderwidth` or `-bd`	Specifies a non-negative value indicating the width of the border to draw around the outside of the window.
`-cursor`	Specifies the mouse cursor to be used for the window.
`-highlightbackground`	Specifies the color to display in the traversal highlight region when the window does not have the input focus.
`-highlightcolor`	Specifies the color to use for the traversal highlight rectangle that is drawn around the window when it has the input focus.
`-highlightthickness`	Specifies a non-negative value indicating the width of the highlight rectangle to draw around the outside of the window.
`-padx`	Specifies a non-negative value indicating how much extra space to request for the window in the X-direction.
`-pady`	Specifies a non-negative value indicating how much extra space to request for the window in the Y-direction.
`-relief`	Specifies the 3D effect desired for the window. Acceptable values are `raised`, `sunken`, `flat`, `ridge`, `solid`, and `groove`.
`-takefocus`	Determines whether or not the window accepts the focus during keyboard traversal.

Standard keywords	Interpretation
`-background`	Specifies the background color to use when drawing.
`-class`	Specifies a class for the window.
`-colormap`	Specifies a color map to use for the window.
`-container`	The value must be a Boolean value. If `true`, it means that this window will be used as a container in which some other application will be embedded (for example, a Tk top level can be embedded using the `-use` keyword). The window will support the appropriate window manager protocols for things such as geometry requests. The window should not have any children of its own in this application. This keyword may not be changed with the configure window command.
`-height`	Specifies the desired height for the window.
`-visual`	Specifies visual information for the new window.
`-width`	Specifies the desired width for the window.

How to do it...

In the following example, we again will create a frame widget with defined keywords to control its appearance. Enter the following command:

```
1 % frame .f -width 160 -height 90 -borderwidth 5 -relief raised
.f

2 % pack .f
```

At this point, your window should look like the following:

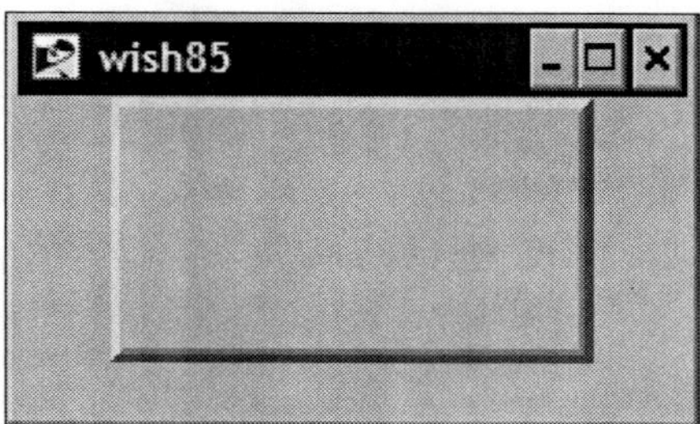

How it works...

Based on the keywords provided, we have created a frame widget named `.f`, a width of `160` pixels, a height of `90` pixels, a border width of `5` pixels, and a `raised` border relief.

Creating a label widget

The Tk **label widget** is used to display information that does not allow direct user input. This information can be any alphanumeric information from simple labels for other controls to large instructions to a user.

The keywords are described in the Tk main pages, as follows:

Standard keyword	Interpretation
`-activebackground`	Specifies the background color to be used when drawing the element. The active background is the color used when the mouse is over the element and when pressing the mouse button will initiate an action.
`-activeforeground`	Specifies the foreground color to be used when drawing the element. The active foreground is the color used when the mouse is over the element and pressing the mouse button will initiate an action.
`-anchor`	Specifies how the information (text, bitmap, and so on) is displayed within the widget. Acceptable values are: `n` – north, top `ne` – northeast, top right `e` – east, right-hand side `se` – southeast, bottom right `s` – south, bottom `sw` – southwest, bottom left `w` – west, left-hand side `nw` – northwest, top right `center` - center
`-background` or `-bg`	Specifies the background color to be used when drawing the element.
`-bitmap`	Specifies a bitmap to display within the element.
`-borderwidth` or `-bd`	Specifies a non-negative value indicating the width of the 3D border to draw around the outside of the window.
`-compound`	Specifies if the widget should display both text and bitmaps/images simultaneously and the placement of where to display the image in relation to the text. Acceptable values are: none, bottom, top, left, right, or center (default).
`-cursor`	Specifies the mouse cursor to be used for the window.
`-disabledforeground`	Specifies the color to use when displaying a disabled element.
`-font`	Specifies the font to use when drawing the element

Standard keyword	Interpretation
-foreground or -fg	Specifies the normal foreground color to be used when drawing the element.
-highlightbackground	Specifies the color to display in the traversal highlight region when the window does not have the input focus.
-highlightcolor	Specifies the color to use for the traversal highlight rectangle that is drawn around the window when it has the input focus.
-highlightthickness	Specifies a non-negative value indicating the width of the highlight rectangle to draw around the outside of the window.
-image	Specifies the image to display within an element. The image must first have been created using the image create command.
-justify	When multiple lines of text exist, this keyword specifies the justification to apply within the element. Acceptable values are: left, center, or right.
-padx	Specifies a non-negative value indicating how much extra space to request for the window in the X-direction
-pady	Specifies a non-negative value indicating how much extra space to request for the window in the Y-direction.
-relief	Specifies the 3D effect desired for the window. Acceptable values are raised, sunken, flat, ridge, solid, and groove.
-takefocus	Determines whether or not the window accepts the focus during keyboard traversal.
-text	Specifies a string to be displayed within the element.
-textvariable	Specifies the name of a text variable that contains text to be displayed within an element.
-underline	Specifies the integer index of a character to be underlined, zero-based.
-wraplength	Specifies the maximum line length at which point the text will be wrapped for those elements that support word wrap.
-height	Specifies the desired height for the window.
-state	Specifies the state of the widget. Acceptable values are normal, active, and disabled.
-width, width, Width	Specifies the desired width for the window.

How to do it...

In the following example, we will create a label with the desired text. Enter the following command:

```
1 % label .l -text "My Label"
```

```
.l

2 % pack .l
```

At this point, your window should look like the following:

How it works...

Based on the keywords provided, we have created a label widget named `.l` containing the text `My Label`.

Creating an entry widget

Perhaps the most commonly used widget for collecting information from the end user is the **entry widget**. The entry widget displays a single-line input area. The widget allows the end user to enter or edit the string within the widget.

The keywords are as follows:

Standard keyword	Interpretation
`-background` or `-bg`	Specifies the background color to be used when drawing the element.
`-borderwidth` or `-bd`	Specifies a non-negative value indicating the width of the 3D border to draw around the outside of the window.
`-cursor`	Specifies the mouse cursor to be used for the window.
`-exportselection`	Specifies if a selection within the widget should also be the X selection. This keyword accepts a Boolean value such as `true`, `false`, `yes`, `no`, `0`, or `1`.
`-font`	Specifies the font to use when drawing the element.
`-foreground` or `-fg`	Specifies the normal foreground color to be used when drawing the element.
`-highlightbackground`	Specifies the color to display in the traversal highlight region when the window does not have the input focus.
`-highlightcolor`	Specifies the color to use for the traversal highlight rectangle that is drawn around the window when it has the input focus.

Standard keyword	Interpretation
`-highlightthickness`	Specifies a non-negative value indicating the width of the highlight rectangle to draw around the outside of the window.
`-insertbackground`	Specifies the color to be used as the background color in the insertion cursor.
`-insertborderwidth`	Specifies a non-negative integer value to indicate the width of the 3D border to draw around the insertion cursor.
`-insertofftime`	Specifies a non-negative integer value to indicate the number of milliseconds the insertion cursor should remain off in each blink cycle. If set to `0` the insertion cursor does not blink.
`-insertontime`	Specifies a non-negative integer value to indicate the number of milliseconds the insertion cursor should remain on in each blink cycle.
`-insertwidth`	Specifies the width of the insertion cursor in pixels.
`-justify`	This keyword is used to specify the justification to apply within the input widget element. Acceptable values are `left`, `center`, or `right`.
`-relief`	Specifies the 3D effect desired for the window. Acceptable values are `raised`, `sunken`, `flat`, `ridge`, `solid`, and `groove`.
`-selectbackground`	Specifies the background color to use for selected items.
`-selectborderwidth`	Specifies the width of the 3D border to draw around selected items.
`-selectforeground`	Specifies the foreground color to use for selected items.
`-takefocus`	Determines whether or not the window accepts the focus during keyboard traversal.
`-textvariable`	Specifies the name of a text variable that contains text to be displayed within an element.
`-xscrollcommand`	Specifies the command to be called during a scroll event. If this value is not set, no command will be executed.
`-height`	Specifies the desired height for the window.
`-state`	Specifies the state of the widget. Acceptable values are `normal`, `active`, and `disabled`.
`-width`	Specifies the desired width for the window.

How to do it...

In the following example, we will create a label with the text desired. Enter the following command:

```
1 % entry .e -borderwidth 3 -width 25
```

```
.e

2 % pack .e
```

At this point, your window should look like the following:

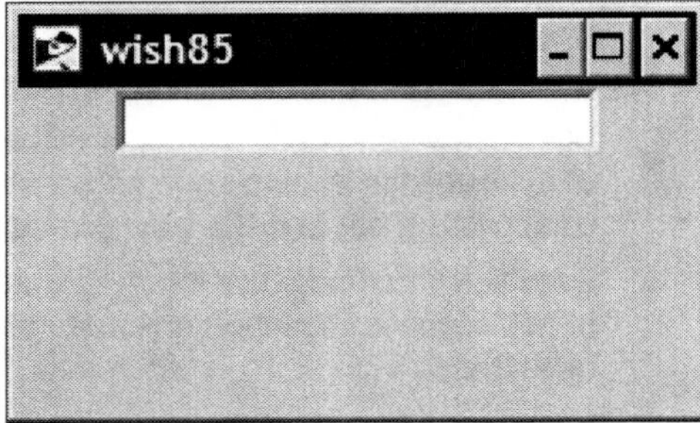

How it works...

Based on the keyword and value pairs provided we have created an entry widget named `.e` with a border width of `3` and a width of `25`. Note that the width is based on the space required to display `25` characters of the font specified or the default font and *not* on screen pixels.

Creating a button widget

Through the button the user is provided with a means to interact with the GUI and our program. This is accomplished through the button's ability to manually execute commands in your application. These actions may be default, as in the `exit` command, or custom procedures that we have written.

The keywords are described in the Tk main pages as follows:

Standard Keywords	Interpretation
`-activebackground`	Specifies the background color to be used when drawing the element. The active background is the color used when the mouse is over the element and when pressing the mouse button will initiate an action.
`-activeforeground`	Specifies the foreground color to be used when drawing the element. The active foreground is the color used when the mouse is over the element and when pressing the mouse button will initiate an action.

Standard Keywords	Interpretation
`anchor`	Specifies how the information (text, bitmap, and so on) is displayed within the widget. Acceptable vales are: `n` - north, top `ne` - northeast, top right `e` - east, right-hand side `se` - southeast, bottom right `s` - south, bottom `sw` - southwest, bottom left `w` - west, left-hand side `nw` - northwest, top right `center` - center
`-background` or `-bg`	Specifies the background color to be used when drawing the element.
`-bitmap`	Specifies a bitmap to display within the element.
`-borderwidth` or `-bd`	Specifies a non-negative value indicating the width of the 3D border to draw around the outside of the window.
`-compound`	Specifies if the widget should display both text and bitmaps/images simultaneously and the placement of where to display the image in relation to the text. Acceptable values are: `none`, `bottom`, `top`, `left`, `right`, or `center` (default).
`-cursor`	Specifies the mouse cursor to be used for the window.
`-disabledforeground`	Specifies the color to use when displaying a disabled element.
`-font`	Specifies the font to use when drawing the element.
`-foreground` or `-fg`	Specifies the normal foreground color to be used when drawing the element.
`-highlightbackground`	Specifies the color to display in the traversal highlight region when the window does not have the input focus.
`-highlightcolor`	Specifies the color to use for the traversal highlight rectangle that is drawn around the window when it has the input focus.
`-highlightthickness`	Specifies a non-negative value indicating the width of the highlight rectangle to draw around the outside of the window.
`-image`	Specifies the image to display within an element. The image must first have been created using the image create command.
`-justify`	When multiple lines of text exist, this keywords specifies the justification to apply within the element. Acceptable values are: `left`, `center`, or `right`.
`-padx`	Specifies a non-negative value indicating how much extra space to request for the window in the X-direction.

Standard Keywords	Interpretation
-pady	Specifies a non-negative value indicating how much extra space to request for the window in the Y-direction.
-relief	Specifies the 3D effect desired for the window. Acceptable values are `raised`, `sunken`, `flat`, `ridge`, `solid`, and `groove`.
-repeatdelay	Specifies the number of milliseconds a key or element must be held down before it will auto-repeat.
-repeatinterval	Used in conjunction with `-repeatdelay`, this keyword specifies the interval between auto-repeats in milliseconds.
-takefocus	Determines whether or not the window accepts the focus during keyboard traversal.
-text	Specifies a string to be displayed within the element.
-textvariable	Specifies the name of a text variable that contains text to be displayed within an element.
-underline	Specifies the integer index of a character to be underlined, zero-based.
-wraplength	Specifies the maximum line length at which point the text will be wrapped for those elements that support word wrap.
-command	Specifies a Tcl command to be activated by a button.
-default	Specifies the default state of the element (See state).
-height	Specifies the desired height for the window.
-overrelief	Specifies an alternate relief for a button to display during mouse-over.
-state	Specifies the state of the widget. Acceptable values are `normal`, `active`, and `disabled`.
-width	Specifies the desired width for the window.

How to do it...

In the following example, we will create a button with specific keywords designed to update the text in a label widget. Enter the following commands:

```
1 % proc updater { } {
      .l configure -text "Updated"
}
2 % label .l -width 70 -borderwidth 3 -text Original
.l


3 % button .b -text Update -command updater
```

```
.b


4 % pack .l -side top
5 % pack .b -side bottom
```

At this point, your window should look like the following:

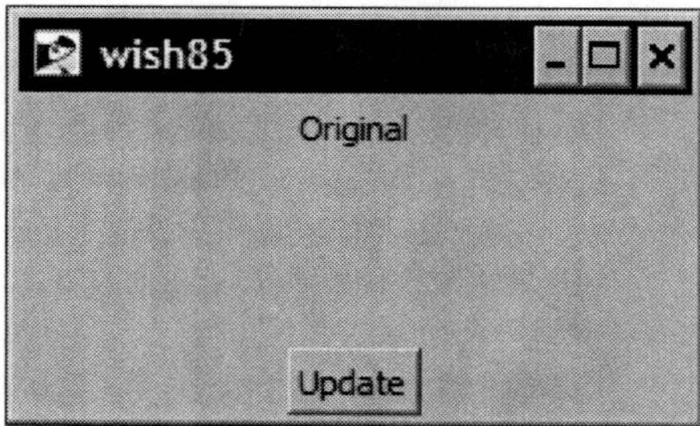

How it works...

Based on the keywords provided, we have created a button widget named `.b` with the text set to `Update` tied to our procedure named `updater`. By clicking the button, we configure the text displayed in the label named `.l` to the string `Updated`.

Creating a listbox widget

The Tk **listbox widget** provides a powerful tool for collecting and displaying string data. Each entry is displayed on an individual line. Elements are added or deleted using the commands inherent to the widget. For screen size consideration, the listbox supports both horizontal and vertical scrolling.

The keywords are described in the Tk main pages as follows:

Standard Keyword	Interpretation
`-background` or `-bg`	Specifies the background color to be used when drawing the element.
`-borderwidth` or `-bd`	Specifies a non-negative value indicating the width of the 3D border to draw around the outside of the window.
`-cursor`	Specifies the mouse cursor to be used for the window.
`-disabledforeground`	Specifies the color to use when displaying a disabled element.
`-exportselection`	Specifies if a selection within the widget should also be the X selection. This keyword accepts a Boolean value such as `true`, `false`, `yes`, `no`, `0`, or `1`.

Standard Keyword	Interpretation
-font	Specifies the font to use when drawing the element.
-foreground or -fg	Specifies the normal foreground color to be used when drawing the element.
-highlightbackground	Specifies the color to display in the traversal highlight region when the window does not have the input focus.
-highlightcolor	Specifies the color to use for the traversal highlight rectangle that is drawn around the window when it has the input focus.
-highlightthickness	Specifies a non-negative value indicating the width of the highlight rectangle to draw around the outside of the window.
-relief	Specifies the 3D effect desired for the window. Acceptable values are raised, sunken, flat, ridge, solid, and groove.
-selectbackground	Specifies the background color to use for selected items.
-selectborderwidth	Specifies the width of the 3D border to draw around selected items.
-takefocus	Determines whether or not the window accepts the focus during keyboard traversal.
-xscrollcommand	Specifies the command to be called during a scroll event. If this value is not set no, command will be executed.
-yscrollcommand	Specifies the command to be called in the event of a scroll event. If this value is not set no, command will be executed.
-activestyle	Specifies the style in which the listbox should be drawn. Acceptable values are: dotbox, none, or underline. Windows default is underline, while dotbox is the default for other operating systems.
-height	Specifies the desired height for the window.
-listvariable	Specifies the name of a variable the value of which will be displayed inside the listbox. If the value changes, the listbox will update automatically.
-selectmode	Specifies the style available for selecting items within a listbox. Acceptable values are: single, browse, multiple or extended. The default is value is browse.
-state	Specifies the state of the widget. Acceptable values are normal, active, and disabled.
-width	Specifies the desired width for the window.

Most widgets have a specific set of commands associated with them. The commands associated with the listbox are presented next, as we will be using the listbox command in the following example. For specific widget commands, please refer to the main pages for each widget.

Commands	Interpretation
`widgetname activate index`	Sets the active element to the one referenced by `index`.
`widgetname bbox index`	Returns a list of four numbers describing the bounding box of the text within the listbox referenced by `index`.
`widgetname cget keyword`	Returns the configuration setting referenced by `keyword`.
`widgetname configure keyword value...`	Configures the `keyword` or `keywords` to the value provided. If no value is provided, this command will return a list containing the keyword and value of the one named keyword.
`widgetname curselection`	Returns a list containing the numeric indices of all the selected elements contained within a listbox.
`widgetname delete first last:`	Deletes one or more elements as referenced by `first` and `last`. If no value for `last` is provided, this will delete a single element.
`widgetname get first last`	Returns the contents of the list as referenced by `first` and `last`. If no value for `last` is provided, the value of a single element is returned.
`widgetname index index`	Returns the integer value corresponding to `index`. If the value for `index` is `end`, this will return a count of all the elements.
`widgetname insert index element...`	Inserts zero or more elements after the `index` referenced by `index`. If the value for `index` is `end`, the data is inserted after the last element.
`widgetname itemcget index keyword`	Returns the item configuration setting referenced by `keyword`.
`widgetname itemconfigure index keyword value...`	This command will query or modify the configuration settings for an item referenced by `index` within the `listbox`. If no value is specified, it will return a list containing the current `keyword` settings. The supported keywords are: `-backgroundcolor`, `-foregroundcolor`, `-selectbackground`, and `-selectforeground`.
`widgetname nearest y`	Based on the coordinates referenced by y, return the visible index of the nearest `listbox` element.

Commands	Interpretation
widgetname scan keywords arguments	Implements scanning of a listbox with one of two forms, based on the keyword referenced. They are: mark x y: Records the current x and y associated with a mouse button press event. Used in conjunction with the scan dragto command below. dragto x y: This command will compute the difference between x and y of the scan mark command and the x and y of the dragto command. It will then adjust the view by ten times the difference between the coordinates giving the appearance of rapidly dragging the list. widgetname see index: Adjusts the view within the listbox to ensure the element referenced by index is visible. widgetname selection keyword argument: This command will adjust the selected element within the listbox based on the keyword provided. The words are as follows: anchor index: Sets the selection anchor to the element referenced by index. If no element exists the index referenced the closed element is anchored. clear first last: Deselects any elements between first and last. includes index: Returns a 1 if the element referenced by index is selected. If not selected, this command will return a 0. set first last: Selects all elements that exist within the range referenced by first and last without affecting the selection of other elements that exist outside of the range.
widgetname size	Returns a decimal string containing a count of the total number of elements contained within a listbox.

Commands	Interpretation
`widgetname xview arguments`	This command is used to query or re-orient the horizontal position of the information contained within the `listbox` window. If no arguments are provided, this command returns a list containing two values representing a real fraction between 0 and 1 that describes the horizontal span currently visible within the window. For example, if the first item is .3 and the second item is .4, then 30% of the list is off-screen to the left, 40% of the list is off-screen to the right, and 30% is visible. The acceptable values are: `index`: Adjust the view so that the character referenced by `index` is displayed at the left side of the window. `moveto fraction`: Adjust the view so that the percentage referenced by `fraction` is off-screen to the left. `scroll number mode`: Shift the view in the window left or right by the amount referenced by `number` in one of the acceptable modes. Acceptable modes are: units (size of character) or pages (screenfuls). If the value contained within `number` is negative, then characters further left become visible; if it is positive, characters further right become visible.
`widgetname yview arguments`	This command is used to query or reorient the vertical position of the information contained within the `listbox` window. If no arguments are provided this command returns a list containing two values representing a real fraction between 0 and 1 that describe the vertical span currently visible within the window. For example if the first item is .3 and the second item is .4 then 30% of the list is off-screen to the top, 40% of the list is off-screen to the bottom and 30% is visible. The acceptable values are: `index`: Adjust the view so that the character referenced by `index` is displayed at the top of the window. `moveto fraction`: Adjust the view so that the percentage referenced by fraction is off-screen to the top. `scroll number mode`: Shift the view in the window up or down by the amount referenced by `number` in one of the acceptable modes. Acceptable modes are: units (lines) or pages (screenfuls). If the value contained within `number` is negative then characters become visible earlier; if positive character become visible later.

How to do it...

In the following example we will create a listbox with specific keywords and add items to the list programmatically, using the `insert` command of the listbox widget. Enter the following commands:

```
1 % listbox .l -borderwidth 3 -height 10 -width 25
pack .l
.l

2 % set x 1
1

3 % while {$x < 10} {
        .l insert end $x;
        incr x;
}
```

At this point, your window should look like the following:

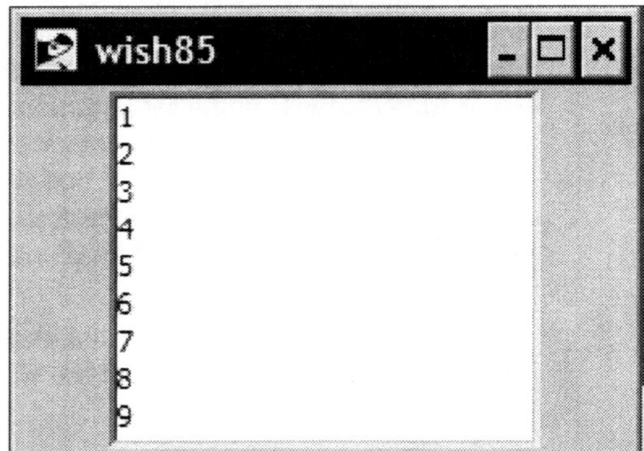

How it works...

Based on the keywords provided we have created a listbox widget named `.l` with a border width of `3`, height of `10` and width of `25`. Using the `listbox insert` command, we have populated the listbox with the desired data.

Creating an image

Before you can display a graphic in Tk, you must first create a Tk image. To accomplish this, Tk provides the `image` command. This command allows you to create, delete, and query the keywords for any of the supported image types. The built-in image types are bitmap (two color graphics) and photo. The photo types as shipped in the base distribution are PPM/PGM and GIF.

Based on the keyword used the image command takes several syntactic forms. The syntax and keywords are as follows:

```
image keyword path
```

Keyword	Interpretation
`create`	Creates an image and a command with the same name.
`delete`	Deletes the named image.
`height`	Returns a decimal string containing the height of the image in pixels.
`inuse`	Returns a Boolean value indicating if the named image provided is currently in use.
`names`	Returns a list containing the names of all created images.
`type`	Returns the type of image as referenced by name.
`types`	Returns a lost containing all valid image types.
`width`	Returns a decimal string containing the width of the image in pixels.

Getting ready

To complete the following example you will need to have a GIF file to select. Please locate the file `tcllogo.gif` in your Tcl installation in the `demos/Tk8.5/images` directory and copy it into your working path.

How to do it…

In the following example we will create an image and display it within a label. Enter the following commands:

```
1 % image create photo image1 -file tcllogo.gif
.image1

2 % label .l -image image1
.l
3 % pack .l
```

At this point, your window should look like the following:

How it works...

In the first step, we have created a Tk image of the type photo that references the file `tcllogo.gif`. Next, we have created a label named `.l` that contains our image.

Creating a simple form

As you can see this selection of widgets allows for a great deal of flexibility and provides enough features to address most of your GUI needs. To illustrate this we will now create a simple form.

How to do it...

In the following example, we will create a listbox with specific keywords and add items to the list programmatically. Using the text editor of your choice create a file named `form.tcl` containing the following text.

```
# Load the TK package
package require Tk

#Procedure to add to the listbox
proc list_add { } {
   set s [ .e get ]
   .l insert end $s
   .e delete 0 end
}
# Create image and widgets
image create photo logo -file tcllogo.gif
```

```
label .logo -image logo
listbox .l -borderwidth 3 -width 25 -height 10
entry .e -width 25
frame .f -width 25 -borderwidth 2 -relief groove
button .f.update -text "Add" -command list_add
button .f.exit -text "Exit" -command exit

# Pack the widgets
pack .logo -side top -anchor w
pack .l -side top -anchor e
pack .f.update -side left
pack .f.exit -side right
pack .f -side bottom -padx 2 -pady 2 -fill both
pack .e -side bottom
```

Now access your program by calling it appropriately for your system. For example:

tclsh85 form.tcl

At this point, your window should look like the following:

Enter the data into the entry box and click the button marked **Add** to update the listbox.

How it works...

The `list_add` procedure gets the string contained in entry widget `e` with the `entry` widget's `get` command and assigns it to a variable `s`. This variable value is inserted into the listbox, after which the entry widget is cleared.

10
Geometry Management

In this chapter, we will cover the following topics:

- Controlling layout with the `pack` command
- Controlling layout with the `grid` command
- Combining `pack` and `grid`
- Creating an address book interface

Introduction

For the purpose of this chapter the term **geometry management** refers to the layout and the design of the interface and not the `wm` command. The GUI is your primary method of interacting with the end user and, as such, is your opportunity to make a good first impression.

Although the specifics of GUI design are not directly covered in this chapter, we need to keep in mind that a poorly designed and executed interface may not only result in frustration for the end user, but also may actually result in the end user looking elsewhere for a solution.

I am sure that you have seen interfaces with bizarre combinations of colors. While they may be the developer's favorite colors in the world, they are not necessarily the best choice for an application. Add in a poor selection for the font colors and you can rapidly create a GUI that is not only shocking to the eye, but also utterly unreadable.

There are many sources available that cover GUI design. Perhaps the most readily available resource though is your own computer. Look at the programs installed on your own system. One thing that you will notice is a similarity in design, color, and layout. Menus at the top, status bar at the bottom, work area easily identifiable, and buttons logically labeled. Now note the coloration. Most programs default to the system default colors as selected by the user. What better way to ensure that the end user is comfortable with the colors selected than using the ones that they have chosen? This not only provides the end user with a level of comfort, but also requires no effort on your part, as this is the default. Additionally, Tk will automatically emulate the window decorations (**Frame**, **Maximize**, **Minimize**, and **Close** buttons) of the operating system. This ensures that the basic look and feel of your application complies with the system that it is operating on.

Unless stated otherwise, we will need to access wish from the command line to complete the following examples. Launch the wish shell appropriately for your operating system and follow the instructions provided in each section.

Controlling layout with the pack command

Tk provides three methods of geometry management—`pack`, `grid`, and the rarely used `place` command. We will be covering the `pack` and `grid` commands. The `pack` command is the basic geometry manager for Tk. When invoked, the `pack` command instructs the packer to arrange the widgets as specified. The **packer** is a geometry manager that arranges the elements of a window in order around the edges. In the following examples, we will see how to use the `pack` command.

Based on the options provided when invoked the `pack` command assumes several forms. The syntactical options are as follows:

Option	Interpretation
`pack widget widget options`	Behaves in the same manner as `pack` configure.
`pack configure widget widget options:`	This command accepts one or more widgets and pairs of options (if desired) to manage the pack. `-after parent`: The parent provided must reference a valid Tk widget. The widget being packed will be loaded after the widget specified. `-anchor position`: The widget will be anchored to the position specified. Acceptable positions are `n`, `ne`, `e`, `se`, `s`, `sw`, `w`, `nw`, or `center` (default). `-before parent`: The parent provided must reference a valid Tk widget. The widget being packed will be loaded before the widget specified. `-expand boolean`: This option instructs the packer to consume the extra space available within the container. Boolean must contain a valid value. `-fill method`: This option instructs the packer to stretch the widget. Acceptable methods are: `none`: Provide the dimensions plus any internal padding, as specified by `-padx` or `-pady` (default). `x`: Stretch the widget to fill all available space along the x axis. `y`: Stretch the widget to fill all available space along the y axis. `both`: Stretch the widget to fill all available space along both the x and y axis. `-in widget`: Insert the widget at the end of the packing order for the widget specified. `-ipadx value`: Specifies the amount of internal horizontal padding to utilize. Value must be a valid screen distance (default value is 0). `-ipady value`: Specifies the amount of internal vertical padding to utilize. Value must be a valid screen distance (default value is 0). `-side location`: Specifies which side of the container to pack against. Acceptable values for location are `top` (default), `bottom`, `left`, and `right`.
`pack forget widget widget`	Remove one or more widgets from the container.
`pack info widget`	Returns a list of the current configuration for the widget specified.

Option	Interpretation
`pack propagate master boolean`	When invoked with a positive Boolean value propagation for master. If invoked with a `false` value, propagation is disabled.
`pack slaves master`	Returns a list of all slave widgets contained within the packing order for master.

How to do it...

In the following example, we will create several labels and arrange them using the `pack` command. Enter the following commands:

```
1 % label .top -background red -text TOP
.top
2 % label .bottom -background red -text BOTTOM
.bottom
3 % label .left -background yellow -text LEFT
.left
4 % label .right -background yellow -text RIGHT
.right
5 % pack .top -side top -fill x
6 % pack .bottom -side bottom -fill x
7 % pack .left -side left -fill y
8 % pack .right -side right -fill y
```

After you resize the window to expose the entirety of the labels, your window should look like the following screenshot:

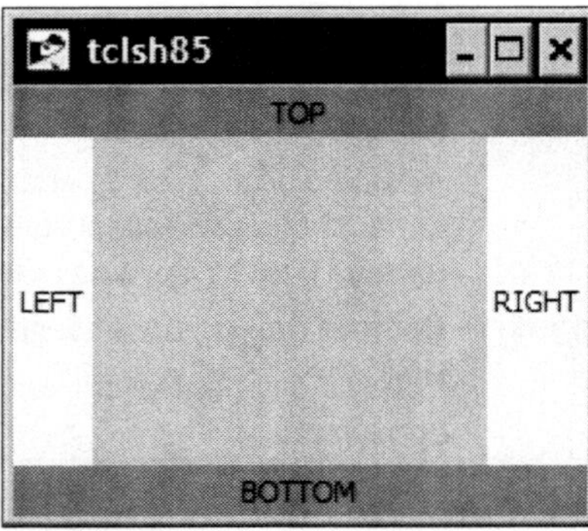

How it works...

The first statement requests that `.top` be put at the top of the window. The `pack` command allocates the top of the window to this widget, and makes it fill the top in the `x` direction. The next statement does the same for the bottom of the window. For `.left`, it takes any remaining space on the left that is not taken up by the `.top` and `.bottom` widgets and allocates that to the `.left` widget in the `y` axis. The next statement does the same for the `.right` widget. While this is a very basic example, I would like to point out some details in regard to the order in which the labels were packed. Note that the `.top` and `.bottom` labels are packed prior to the `.left` and `.right` labels. As such, they fill the total top and bottom of the window, while the left and right are contained within the confines of the top and bottom. Had we packed `.left` and `.right` first, the `x` fill regions would be bounded by the `y` regions, as shown in the following image. This illustrates the importance of correct ordering of the packing of widgets.

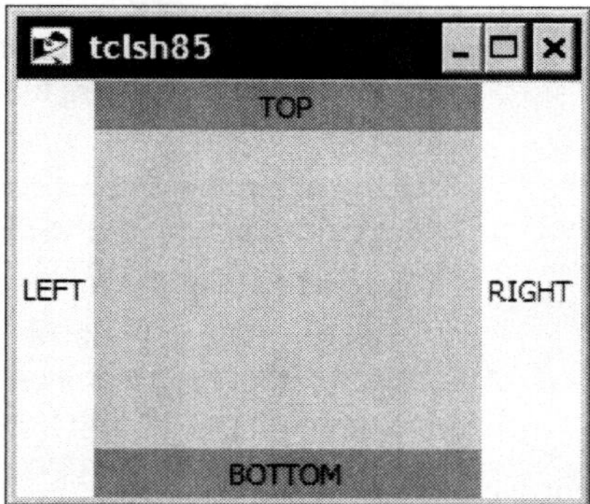

Controlling layout with the grid command

Care must be taken in packing the widgets to ensure that the desired layout is obtained. The `pack` command provides a convenient method of geometry management for simple forms. However, for more complex forms, the `grid` command allows you to manage your widget placement by creating and configuring rows and columns for widget placement.

To illustrate this better, think of the grid as being similar to a table or a spreadsheet, as it contains rows and columns, as follows:

	Column 0	Column 1	Column 2
Row 0			
Row 1			
Row 2			

Please note that the column and row numbering are zero-based. This is the grid layout that we will use in the following example.

Based on the options provided, when invoked, the `grid` command assumes several forms. The syntactical options are as follows:

Option	Interpretation
`grid widget row column`	Behaves in the same manner as grid configure.
`grid anchor parent anchor`	Controls placement of the grid itself. Acceptable values are `n`, `ne`, `e`, `se`, `s`, `sw`, `w`, or `nw` (default).
`grid bbox parent column1 row1 column2 row2`	When no arguments are provided this command will return the size of the bounding box in pixels as a four digit integer. The first two are the pixel offset for the top-left corner from the parent. The second two are the size of the bounding box (width and height). If a single column and row are provided, the bounding box for the individual cell is returned. If two column and row pairs are provided the values for the bounding box spanning the rows is returned.
`grid columnconfigure parent column option value`	Query or set the properties of the column referenced for the parent provided. The valid options are: `-minsize`: Set the minimum size for the column. `-weight`: Set the relative weight for assigning extra space within the column. A value of 0 indicates that the column will not deviate from its defined size. A positive value determines the rate at which the column will increase in size. `-uniform`: When a value is supplied, the column is placed into a group with other defined columns. All the members of the group have their space allocated in strict proportion to their `-weight` value. `-pad`: Specifies the number of screen units to be added to the largest widget contained within a column. If no value is specified the current value is returned. If only the parent and column are provided all current settings are returned in a list containing option/value pairs.

Option	Interpretation
`grid configure widget options`	Accepts one or more widgets followed by option/value pairs to configure. Acceptable values are: `-column n`: Insert the widget such that it occupies the column referenced by n. If this option is not utilized the widget is placed to the right of the previous widget configured by the command. `-columnspan n`: Insert the widget such that it occupies n columns. `-in parent`: Place the widget within the parent referenced. For example, placing a button within a frame. `-ipadx value`: Specifies the amount of internal horizontal padding to utilize. Value must be a valid screen distance (default value is 0). `-ipady value`: Specifies the amount of internal vertical padding to utilize. Value must be a valid screen distance (default value is 0). `-row n`: Insert the widget such that it occupies the row referenced by n. If this option is not utilized the widget is placed on the same row as the last widget configured by the command. `-rowspan n`: Insert the widget such that it occupies n rows. `-sticky style`: Used to configure placement of the widget within a cell in the event the cell is larger than the widget. Style accepts a string containing 0 or more of the `n`, `s`, `e`, or `w` characters as well as optional spaces or commas. If `ns` or `ew` are specified, the widget will be stretched to occupy the entire height or width of the cell as appropriate. Default placement is at the center of the cell.
`grid forget widget widget`	Remove one or more widgets from the grid. Configuration values for the widget specified are discarded. If the widget is then returned to the grid all desired configurations must be specified.
`grid info widget`	Returns a list containing the option/value pairs for the current configuration of the widget referenced.
`grid location parent x y`	Based on the screen location as referenced by `x` and `y` this command returns the column and row number. For locations above and left of the grid a -1 is returned.

Option	Interpretation
`grid remove widget widget`	Remove one or more widgets from the grid. Configuration values for the widget specified are not discarded. If the widget is then returned to the grid, all the desired configuration is reapplied.
`grid size parent`	Returns the size of the grid as column the row.
`grid slaves master option value`	If no options are provided, this command will return a list of all widgets contained within master. The acceptable values for option are `-row` or `-column`. If these values are provided, only those widgets in the row or column referenced are returned.

How to do it...

In the following example, we will create several widgets and arrange them using the `grid` command. Enter the following commands:

```
1 % entry .e -width 10
.e

2 % label .1 -text ONE
.1

3 % label .2 -text TWO
.2

4 % label .3 -text THREE
.3

5 % button .b -text Exit -command exit
.b

6 % grid .e -row 0 -column 2
7 % grid .1 -row 1 -column 0
8 % grid .2 -row 1 -column 1
9 % grid .3 -row 1 -column 2
10 % grid .b -row 2 -column 2
```

At this point, your window should look like the following:

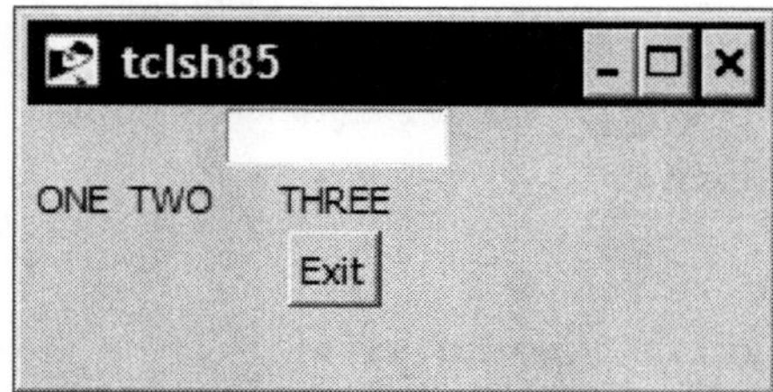

How it works...

Based on the placement instructions passed to the `grid` command, we have placed our widgets at various locations within the grid as illustrated in the following table:

	Column 0	Column 1	Column 2
Row 0			Entry Widget
Row 1	Label	Label	Label
Row 2			Button

Combining pack and grid

It is not possible to combine `pack` and `grid` within the same container. If you attempt this the geometry managers will both attempt to control the screen geometry resulting in the screen failing to load. If you choose to combine the two, you may use `pack` to display a container (for example, a frame), which then utilizes the `grid` command to place the widgets within a grid located within the frame.

How to do it...

In the following example, we will create a frame and load it using the `pack` command. We will then arrange several widgets using the `grid` command identical to the previous example whose parent is the frame. Enter the following commands:

```
1 % frame .f -borderwidth 3 -relief raised
.f

2 % entry .f.e -width 10
.f.e

3 % label .f.1 -text ONE
```

```
.f.1

4 % label .2 -text TWO
.f.2

5 % label .f.3 -text THREE
.f.3

6 % button .f.b -text Exit -command exit
.f.b

7 % pack .f
8 % grid .f.e -row 0 -column 2
9 % grid .f.1 -row 1 -column 0
10 % grid .f.2 -row 1 -column 1
11 % grid .f.3 -row 1 -column 2
12 % grid .f.b -row 2 -column 2
```

At this point, your window should look like the following:

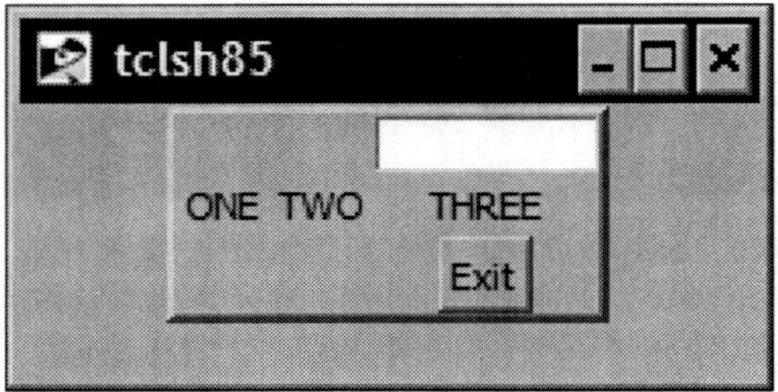

How it works...

We are able to combine the two geometry managers due to the fact that the container of the frame is the window itself, while the container of the grid is the frame. In this manner, the geometry managers are not competing for control of the geometry.

Creating an address book interface

In the following example, we will create an **address book** interface containing button, entry, label, and frame widgets. This will be the basis for the final application and illustrate how to use the `grid` and `pack` commands to create a more complex layout. The interface design is as follows:

<table>
<tr><th></th><th>Column 0</th><th>Column 1</th><th>Column 2</th><th>Column 3</th></tr>
<tr><td>Row 0</td><td>First Name Entry</td><td colspan="2">Last Name Entry</td><td rowspan="7">Photo Label</td></tr>
<tr><td>Row 1</td><td>First Name Label</td><td colspan="2">Last Name Label</td></tr>
<tr><td>Row 2</td><td colspan="3">Address Entry</td></tr>
<tr><td>Row 3</td><td colspan="3">Address Label</td></tr>
<tr><td>Row 4</td><td>City Entry</td><td>State Entry</td><td>Zip Entry</td></tr>
<tr><td>Row 5</td><td>City Label</td><td>State Label</td><td>Zip Label</td></tr>
<tr><td>Row 6</td><td colspan="2">Phone Entry</td><td></td></tr>
<tr><td>Row 7</td><td colspan="2">Phone Label</td><td></td><td>Photo Label</td></tr>
<tr><td>Row 8</td><td>Previous Button</td><td></td><td>Next Button</td><td></td></tr>
<tr><td>Row 9</td><td>Add Button</td><td>Save Button</td><td>Delete Button</td><td>Exit Button</td></tr>
</table>

Getting ready

To complete the following example, open the text editor of your choice and enter the following text. Then save the file in your path with the name `address_book.tcl`.

```
# Load the Tk Package
package require Tk

# Main Frame
frame .main -borderwidth 1 -relief solid -padx 10 -pady 10

# Entry Widgets
entry .main.efirst -width 25
entry .main.elast -width 25
entry .main.eaddress -width 50
entry .main.ecity -width 25
entry .main.estate -width 3
entry .main.ezip -width 5
entry .main.ephone -width 25

# Label Widgets
label .main.first -text "First Name"
label .main.last -text "Last Name"
label .main.address -text "Address"
label .main.city -text "City"
label .main.state -text "ST"
label .main.zip -text "Zip"
label .main.phone -text "Phone"
label .main.photo -text "Photo" -width 15

# Frame for Photo Widget
```

```
label .main.picture -width 120 -height 160 -borderwidth 3 -background
black

# Button Widgets
button .main.previous -text "Previous" -width 15
button .main.next -text "Next" -width 15
button .main.add -text "Add" -width 15
button .main.save -text "Save" -width 15
button .main.delete -text "Delete" -width 15
button .main.exit -text "Exit" -width 15 -command exit

# Pack Command
pack .main

# Grid command
grid .main.efirst -row 0 -column 0 -sticky nw
grid .main.elast -row 0 -column 1 -columnspan 2 -sticky nw
grid .main.picture -row 0 -column 3 -rowspan 7 -sticky nw
grid .main.first -row 1 -column 0 -sticky nw
grid .main.last -row 1 -column 1 -columnspan 2 -sticky nw
grid .main.eaddress -row 2 -column 0 -columnspan 3 -sticky nw
grid .main.address -row 3 -column 0 -columnspan 3 -sticky nw
grid .main.ecity -row 4 -column 0 -sticky nw
grid .main.estate -row 4 -column 1 -sticky nw
grid .main.ezip -row 4 -column 2 -sticky nw
grid .main.city -row 5 -column 0 -sticky nw
grid .main.state -row 5 -column 1 -sticky nw
grid .main.zip -row 5 -column 2 -sticky nw
grid .main.ephone -row 6 -column 0 -columnspan 2 -sticky nw
grid .main.phone -row 7 -column 0 -columnspan 2 -sticky nw
grid .main.photo -row 7 -column 3 -sticky nw
grid .main.previous -row 8 -column 0 -sticky ne
grid .main.next -row 8 -column 2 -sticky nw
grid .main.add -row 9 -column 0 -sticky ne
grid .main.save -row 9 -column 1 -sticky nw
grid .main.delete -row 9 -column 2 -sticky nw
grid .main.exit -row 9 -column 3 -sticky nw
```

How to do it...

Launch your program by calling the program from the Tcl shell, as appropriate for your platform:

tclsh85 addressbook.tcl

At this point, your window should look like the following screenshot:

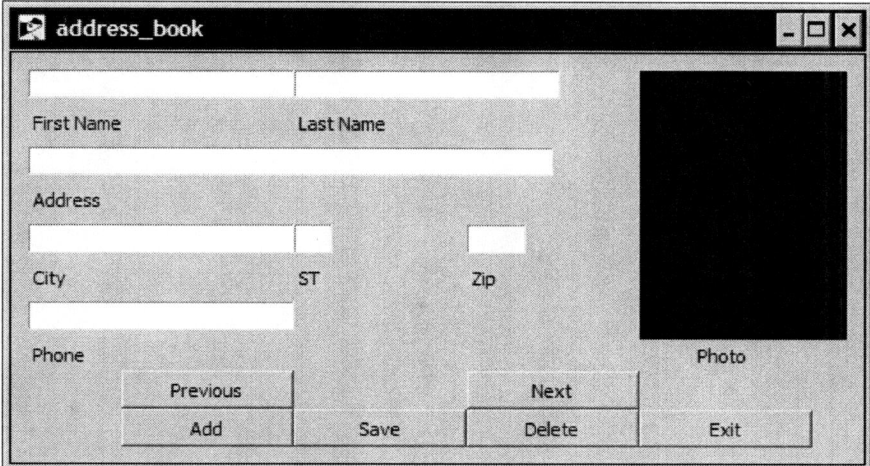

How it works...

We have used the `pack` command to display the `.main` frame. By assigning the widgets proper rows and columns as defined in our interface design, we obtained a form that matches the desired layout.

11
Using Tcl Built-in Dialog Windows

In this chapter, we will cover:

- Displaying a message box
- Displaying a confirmation dialog
- Displaying the color picker
- Displaying the directory dialog
- Displaying the file selection dialog
- Selecting a directory and file

Introduction

Thankfully, we are not limited to dialog windows of our own creation. Tk provides a full suite of predefined **dialog windows** to assist us in the more common tasks of collecting, notifying, and general interactions with the end user. These dialog windows allow us to rapidly create an interface that is both professional in appearance and familiar in functionality with minimum effort. As with all Tk-based windows, the appearance of the native OS is duplicated automatically.

Although you are displaying a full graphical window, the dialog windows are invoked in the same manner as a Tcl command. As such, to assign the return values from the various dialog windows to a variable, you must utilize the `set` command in conjunction with the dialog commands.

Unless otherwise stated, we will need to access wish from the command line to complete the following examples. Launch the wish shell appropriately for your operating system and follow the instructions provided in each section.

Displaying a message box

The `tk_messageBox` command displays a message window with a defined message, an icon and a collection of command buttons and waits on the user's response. The return value provided is the symbolic value (see the `-type` option in the following table) assigned to the button selected.

The syntax is as follows:

```
tk_messageBox option value …
```

The `tk_messageBox` command accepts one or more `option value` pairs as detailed below. If no option value pairs are provided the command will display an empty window with an **OK** button.

Option	Interpretation
`-default name`	Designates which button is the default.
`-detail string`	Displays a secondary message to the message provided by the `-message` option.
`-icon name`	Sets the icon to display, based on the value referenced by name. Acceptable values are: `error`, `info` (default), `question`, or `warning`.
`-message string`	Sets the message to be displayed
`-parent window`	Specifies the parent of the dialog. The dialog is displayed on top of the parent.
`-title string`	Sets the text to be displayed in the dialog title bar.
`-type name`	Specifies the button set to be utilized by the dialog. Acceptable values are:
	`abortretryignore`: Displays three buttons with the symbolic names abort, retry, and ignore.
	`ok`: Displays a single button with the symbolic name ok.
	`okcancel`: Displays two buttons with the symbolic names ok and cancel.
	`retrycancel`: Displays two buttons with the symbolic names retry and cancel.
	`yesno`: Displays two buttons with the symbolic names yes and no.
	`yesnocancel`: Displays three buttons with the symbolic names yes, no, and cancel.

How to do it...

In the following example, we will display a message box and assign the return value to a named variable. Enter the following commands:

```
1 % set response [tk_messageBox -message "Confirm Exit" -icon question -type okcancel -detail "Please select \"OK\" to exit"
```

You should now see the following dialog displayed.

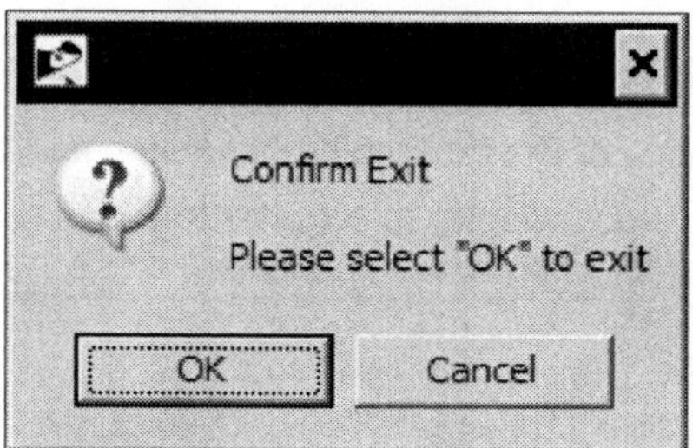

Note that in your shell window, the input line is no longer active and if this dialog were being displayed from an application, we could no longer interact with any other widgets in the same application. This is due to the fact that the application (in this case, the wish shell) is awaiting a response. Click on the **OK** button and you will notice that the symbolic value of `ok` is displayed on the command line and you can now interact with your shell. Enter the following command to confirm that the symbolic value was assigned to the named variable:

```
2 % puts $response
ok
```

How it works...

Based on the option value pairs provided, Tk has displayed a `tk_messageBox` with the messages and buttons desired. On completion, the return value of the button selected was assigned to a named variable.

Displaying a confirmation dialog

The `tk_dialog` command displays a modal message window and awaits the user's response. The value returned provides the index of the button selected: 0 for the leftmost; with the value increasing by 1 for each additional button. If the dialog is destroyed prior to the user making a selection, the return value is -1. All arguments must be provided.

The syntax is as follows:

```
tk_dialog window title text bitmap default string…
```

Option	Interpretation
window	Name to assign to the dialog (for example `confirmDialog`).
title	Sets the text to be displayed in the dialog title bar.
text	Sets the message to be displayed
bitmap	Sets the bitmap (icon) to be displayed in the top of the dialog to the left of the text. If an empty string is passed no bitmap will be displayed.
default	Designates which button is default. This may have an effect on the visual appearance of the buttons and can also be tied to the <return> key.
string	Sets the text to display in each button from left to right. One button will be displayed for each string provided.

How to do it...

In the following example, we will display a dialog box and assign the return value to a named variable. Enter the following commands:

```
1 % set response [tk_dialog .my_dialog "Confirmation" "Do you wish to
proceed?" "" 0 Yes No "Maybe Later"]
```

You should now see the following dialog displayed, as shown next:

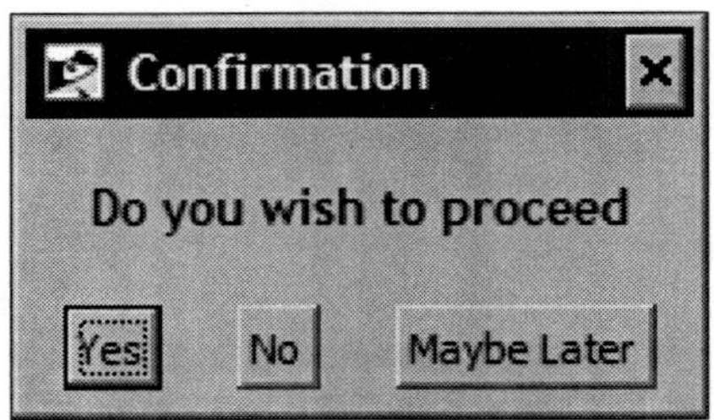

Note that in your shell window the input line is no longer active. This is due to the fact that the application (in this case the wish shell) is awaiting a response. Click on the **No** button and you will notice that the return value of `1` is displayed on the command line and you can now interact with your shell. Enter the following command to confirm that the index value was assigned to the named variable:

```
2 % puts $response
1
```

How it works...

Based on the option value pairs provided, Tk has displayed a `tk_dialog` with multiple buttons, each displayed with defined string values. On completion, the dialog has returned the index value of the button selected and that value was assigned to a named variable.

Displaying the color picker

The `tk_chooseColor` command displays a dialog window that allows the user to select a color. The actual appearance of the color picker will vary, based on the display manager in use. The return hexadecimal value of the color selected is returned. If the user clicks on the **Cancel** button, an empty string is returned.

The syntax is as follows:

```
tk_chooseColor option value ...
```

The `tk_chooseColor` command accepts one or more `option value` pairs as detailed in the following table. If no option value pairs are provided, the command will display a dialog with the default values.

Option	Interpretation
`-initialcolor color`	Sets the starting color to display in the color picker.
`-parent window`	Specifies the parent of the dialog. The dialog is displayed on top of the parent.
`-title string`	Sets the text to be displayed in the dialog title bar.

How to do it...

In the following example, we will create a frame and then display a color picker dialog and assign the return value to our frame as the background color. Enter the following commands:

```
1 % frame .f -width 250 -height 250 -borderwidth 3 -background white
.f

2 % pack .f
3 % .f configure -background [tk_chooseColor -initialcolor gray -title
"Pick A Color"]
```

You should see the Tk window with the frame `.f` displayed following the second command line entry. After you enter the third command line, you will see the color picker dialog (refer to the next screenshot):

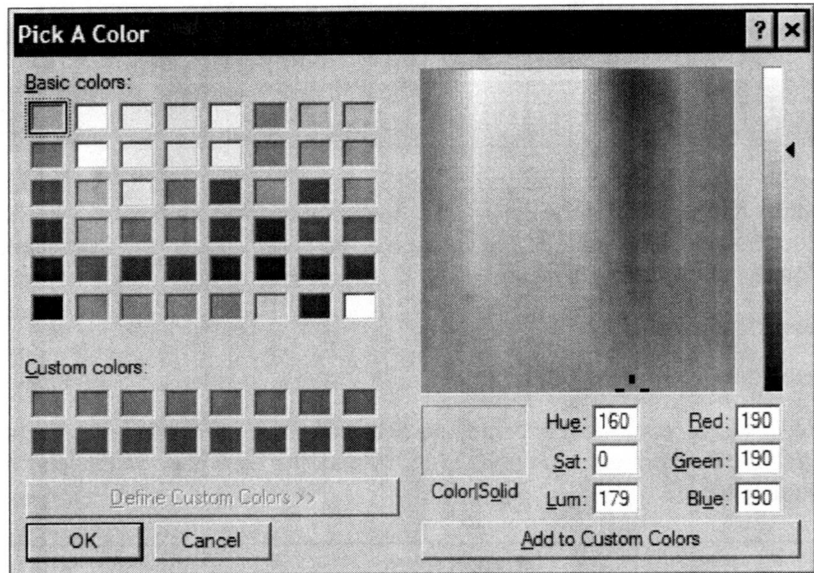

Note that in your shell window, the input line is no longer active. This is due to the fact that the application (in this case, the wish shell) is awaiting a response. Select a color and click on the **OK** button and you will see that the background color of your frame has been changed to the color selected.

How it works...

Based on the option value pairs provided, Tk has displayed a `tk_chooseColor` dialog. When a color has been selected, the value is returned; in this case, to the configure command for the frame widget.

Displaying the directory dialog

The `tk_chooseDirectory` command displays a dialog window that allows the end user to select a directory, as the name implies. The return value is the absolute directory path selected or an empty string (if the **Cancel** button is clicked).

The syntax is as follows:

```
tk_chooseDirectory option value …
```

The `tk_chooseDirectory` command accepts one or more `option value` pairs as detailed below. If no option value pairs are provided, the command will display the default values for the dialog.

Option	Interpretation
`-initialdir directory`	Sets the initial directory to display. If not set, the current working directory will be displayed.
`-mustexist boolean`	Specifies if the user may specify a non-existing directory.
`-parent window`	Specifies the parent of the dialog. The dialog is displayed on top of the parent.
`-title string`	Sets the text to be displayed in the dialog title bar.

How to do it...

In the following example, we will display a message box and assign the return value to a named variable. Enter the following commands:

```
1 % set response [tk_chooseDirectory -initialdir ~ -title "Select a
Directory"]
```

You should now see a similar dialog displayed, based on your display manager.

Note that in your shell window, the input line is no longer active. This is due to the fact that the application (in this case, the wish shell) is awaiting a response. Select a directory (in this case I have selected my home directory) and click on the **OK** button and you will notice that full path for the directory selected is displayed. Enter the following command to confirm that the symbolic value was assigned to the named variable:

```
2 % puts $response
C:/Documents and Settings/Bert
```

How it works...

Based on the option value pairs provided, Tk has displayed a `tk_chooseDirectory` with the messages and buttons desired. On completion, the return value was assigned to a named variable.

Displaying the file selection dialog

The `tk_getOpenFile` and `tk_getSaveFile` commands both display a dialog window that allows the end user to select a file to either be opened or saved. The `tk_getOpenFile` is used for selecting an existing file only. The `tk_getSaveFile` is similar to the Windows **Save As** dialog box and allows a user to specify a name or select an existing file. If an existing file is selected, the end user is automatically prompted to confirm if the existing file may be overwritten. If the **Cancel** button is selected, an empty string is returned.

The syntaxes are as follows:

```
tk_getOpenFile option value …
tk_getSaveFile option value …
```

Both commands accept one or more `option value` pair(s), as detailed in the following table. If no option value pairs are provided, the command will display the default values for the dialog.

Option	Interpretation
`-defaultextension extension`	This is used to specify a string to be appended to the filename if the filename provided has no extension.
`-filetypes pattern`	If the platform supports a file type listbox, this option is used to set those file types desired. If the file types listbox is not supported or this value is not specified all file types are displayed. These are passed as a list of the form: `{{typename} {extension}}`

Option	Interpretation
`-initialdir directory`	Sets the initial directory to display. If not set, the current working directory will be displayed.
`-initialfile filename`	Sets the initial filename to be displayed.
`-message string`	Specifies a message to display in the dialog. (MAC OS X only)
`-multiple boolean`	If `true`, this allows for selection of multiple files.
`-parent window`	Specifies the parent of the dialog. The dialog is displayed on top of the parent.
`-title string`	Sets the text to be displayed in the dialog title bar.
`-typevariable variable`	If defined, this must contain a global variable to be used to set the default filter to use in the file types listbox.

How to do it...

In the following example, we define a file type to be used when we display a dialog box and assign the return value to a named variable. Enter the following commands:

```
1 % set types {
  {{Text Files} {.txt}}
  {{Rich Text} {.rtf}}
  {{All Files}  *}
}

2 % set response [tk_getOpenFile -filetypes $types]
```

You should now see the following dialog displayed:

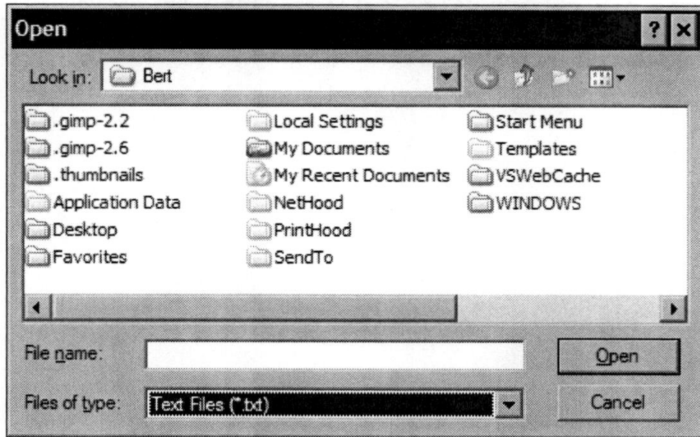

Note that in your shell window the input line is no longer accessible. This is due to the fact that the application (in this case the wish shell) is awaiting a response. Select a file (in this case `break.tcl`) and click on the **Open** button and you will notice that full path for the file selected is displayed. Enter the following command to confirm that the symbolic value was assigned to the named variable:

```
3 % puts $response
C:/Documents and Settings/Bert/break.tcl
```

How it works...

Based on the option value pairs provided, Tk has displayed a `tk_getOpenFile` with the file types desired. When activated, the return value was assigned to a named variable.

Selecting a directory and file

In the following example, we will see how simple it is to combine the functionality of the `tk_chooseDirectory` dialog (which returns only a directory listing) with the `tk_getOpenFile` dialog (which returns a full file path) to assign the directory in use and the file selected to separate variables. This will be accomplished by the Tcl file command in combination with the `tk_getOpenFile` dialog. I use this to allow a user to select or define a configuration file and default directory without requiring the use of two separate dialogs.

How to do it...

In the following example we display a File Selection dialog box and assign the return value to a named variable as well as strip out the directory and assign this to a second named variable. Enter the following commands:

```
1 % set response [tk_getOpenFile -filetypes $types]
```

You should now see the following dialog displayed.

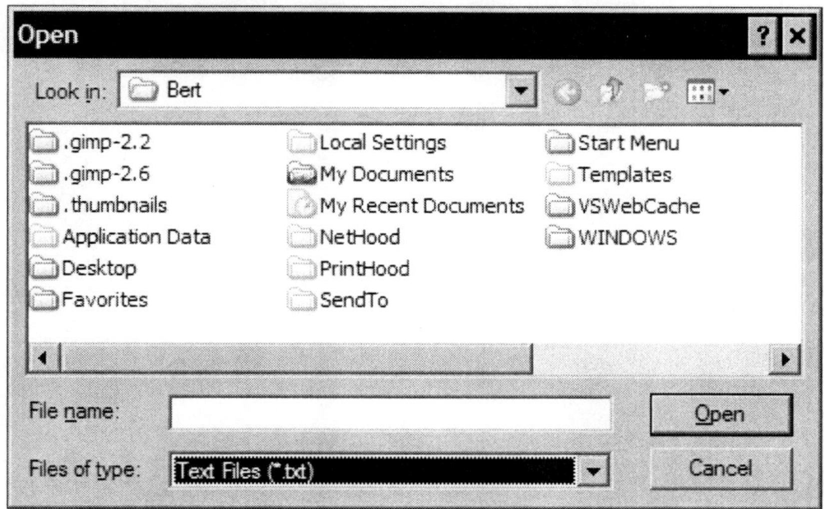

Note that in your shell window the input line is no longer active. This is due to the fact that the application (in this case the wish shell) is awaiting a response. Select a file and click on the **Open** button and you will notice that the full path for the file selected is displayed. Enter the following command to assign the directory path to the second named variable:

```
2 % set my_directory [file dirname $response]
C:/Documents and Settings/Bert


3 % puts "$response $my_directory"
C:/Documents and Settings/Bert/break.tcl C:/Documents and Settings/Bert
```

How it works...

Based on the option value pairs provided, Tk has displayed a `tk_getOpenFile` with the file types desired, as in a previous example. On completion, the return value was assigned to a named variable and by utilizing the `file` command, we were able to isolate the directory at the same time.

12
Creating and Managing Menus

In this chapter, we will cover the following topics:

- Creating a menu
- Adding menu buttons
- Displaying a pop-up menu
- Data entry application

Introduction

Menus are an integral part of the Graphical User Interface (GUI). Most GUI-based applications contain a menu and follow a standard layout and implementation. By following the standard presentation of a menu, we can provide our users with an effective and familiar interface. But what is the standard?

Thankfully, there are numerous standards available to assist in the design and layout of a menu. IEEE, US Government provides requirements for accessibility, language-specific documents, and others provide numerous examples of menu design and these are readily available in print or online. As always, the programs on your computer are an invaluable resource. The companies that sell these programs have invested hundreds of hours and vast amounts of money to ensure that their menus are compliant with the standards.

Unless otherwise stated, we will need to create a text file containing the commands provided within the recipes. To complete the following example, open the text editor of your choice and enter the text that follows the recipe. Then save the file in your path with the name `my_menu.tcl`.

Creating a menu

In Tk the menu is not just a name for a part of your GUI, but also the actual widget command name as well. The `menu` command will create a new menu widget.

The syntax is as follows:

```
menu name option value…
```

The `menu` command accepts one or more `option value` pairs, as detailed in the following table:

Option	Interpretation
`-accelerator`	Specifies an accelerator or keyboard hotkeys to be displayed to the right-hand side of the menu text. The specific acceptable values are dependent on the display manager in use. For example, in a Windows application, *Control+N* would be an acceptable value.
`-activebackground`	Specifies the background color to be used when drawing the element. The active background is the color used when the mouse is over the element and when pressing the mouse button will initiate an action.
`-activeborderwidth`	Specifies the width of the 3D border to draw around the active item.
`-activeforeground`	Specifies the foreground color to be used when drawing the element. The active foreground is the color used when the mouse is over the element and when pressing the mouse button will initiate an action.
`-background` or `-bg`	Specifies the background color to be used when drawing the element.
`-borderwidth` or `-bd`	Specifies a non-negative value indicating the width of the 3D border to draw around the outside of the window.
`-cursor`	Specifies the mouse cursor to be used for the window.
`-disabledforeground`	Specifies the color to use when displaying a disabled element.
`-font`	Specifies the font to use when drawing the element.
`-foreground` or `-fg`	Specifies the normal foreground color to be used when drawing the element.
`-relief`	Specifies the 3D effect desired for the window. Acceptable values are `raised`, `sunken`, `flat`, `ridge`, `solid`, and `groove`.
`-takefocus`	Determines whether or not the window accepts the focus during keyboard traversal.

Option	Interpretation
`-postcommand`	If specified, this provides a command to execute each time the menu is posted.
`-selectcolor`	Specifies the color to display as the background for menus containing check or radio buttons when they are selected.
`-tearoff`	This option accepts a Boolean value and specifies if a menu should include a tear-off entry. A `tearoff` entry allows the user to detach the menu item and display it independent of the menu.
`-tearoffcommand`	If specified, this provides a command to execute each time the menu is torn off.
`-title`	Specifies the title to display for the window created if a menu is torn off. If not specified, the window title will display the label for the top level menu item.
`-type`	Specifies the type of menu. Acceptable values are `menubar`, `tearoff`, or `normal`.

Creation of the `menu` widget additionally created a new Tcl command of the same name. These commands are accessed using the following syntax:

```
name command arguments
```

Several of the menu commands accept an argument to indicate which menu entry to affect. These are referred to as the indexes and may be specified in any of the following manners. Note that those items displayed in italics are not keywords but indicate a specific numeric or textual value placeholder.

Index	Interpretation
number	A numeric designation of the index with a base of 0.
`active`	The menu item that is currently active.
`end`	Last entry in a menu.
`last`	Last entry in a menu.
`none`	Normally used with the activate command, this is used to deactivate all menu items.
@number	When utilized in this manner, the number is treated as a y-coordinate and the entry closest to the coordinate is used.
pattern	Used to perform pattern matching on the label of each entry when none of the above index methods is sufficient.

The commands are as follows:

Specific commands	Interpretation
`name activate index`	Set the menu item at index to activated.
`name add type option value...`	This command adds a new menu item at the bottom of the menu. The type of entry is specified by `type`. The acceptable values for type are `cascade`, `checkbutton`, `command`, `radiobutton`, or `separator`. Additional arguments are specified as an option/value pair, as detailed below: `-activebackground value`: Specifies a background color to display when the item is active. `-activeforeground value`: Specifies a foreground color to display when the item is active. `-accelerator value`: Specifies a string to display at the right side of the menu item. Normally, used to display a keyboard shortcut. This is not available for `separator` or `tearoff` items. `-background value`: Specifies a background color to display when the item is in a normal state. `-bitmap value`: Specifies a bitmap to display in the menu instead of a textual label. This is not available for `separator` or `tearoff` items. `-columnbreak value`: When set to 0, the entry appears below the previous entry. When set to 1, the item appears at the top of a new column. `-command value`: Specifies a Tcl command to execute when the menu item is activated. `-compound value`: Specifies if the menu should display both an image and text and where the image should be displayed. Acceptable values are `bottom`, `center`, `left`, `none` (default), `right`, or `top`. `-font value`: Specifies the font to use when displaying the item. `-foreground value`: Specifies the foreground color to use for displaying the menu item. `-hidemargin value`: Specifies whether or not the standard margins should be drawn for this menu. The 0 indicates that the margin is used, 1 indicates that it is not. `-image value`: Specifies an image to display in place of a bitmap or textual label. This is not available for `separator` or `tearoff` items. `-indicatoron value`: Only applies to checkbox or radio button items. Accepts a Boolean value.

Specific commands	Interpretation
	`-label value`: Specifies a string to display for the item. This is not available for `separator` or `tearoff` items. `-menu value`: Cascade items only. Specifies the name for the submenus associated with this item. `-offvalue value`: Check button only. Specifies the value to store in the item's associated variable when the entry is deselected. `-onvalue value`: Check button only. Specifies the value to store in the item's associated variable when the entry is deselected. `-selectcolor value`: Check button and radio button only. Specifies the color to display when the item is selected. `-selectimage value`: Check button and radio button only. Specifies an image to display in place of the default image when the item is selected. `-state value`: Specifies the state of the item. Acceptable values are `normal`, `active` or `disabled`. This is not available for `separator` items. `-underline value`: Specifies the index of a character in the label to underline as a keyboard accelerator. This index is 0 based and is not available for `separator` or `tearoff` items. `-value value`: Radio button only. Specifies the value to store in the item's variable when the item is selected. `-variable value`: Check button and radio button only. Specifies the name of a global variable to store the value for the item.
`name cget option`	Returns the current configuration value for the `option` specified.
`name clone newname type`	Create a clone of the menu with the name as specified in `newname` of the type `normal`, `menubar`, or `tearoff`. Changes to one menu propagate to the other and are bidirectional.
`name configure option value...`	Query or modify the `option` of the menu.
`name delete index1 index2`	Delete all menu items between `index1` and `index2` inclusive. If no value is passed for `index2`, only the item at `index1` is deleted.
`name entrycget index option`	Returns the current configuration value for the `option` specified for the item at `index`.
`name entryconfigure index options`	Query or modify the `option` of the menu item specified at `index`.
`name index index`	Returns the index for the corresponding `index`.
`name insert index type option value...`	This is the same as the add command except it inserts a new item after the item located at index.

Specific commands	Interpretation
`name invoke index`	Invoke the action for the item specified by `index`.
`name post x y`	Display the menu at the coordinates provided by `x` and `y`.
`name postcascade index`	Display the submenu associated with the cascade item specified by `index` and unpost any previously displayed submenus.
`name type index`	Returns the type of item as specified by `index`.
`name unpost`	Remove the menu from display. Not available on Windows or Macintosh.
`name xposition index`	Returns the x-coordinate of the leftmost pixel in the item specified in `index`.
`name yposition index`	Returns the y-coordinate of the leftmost pixel in the item specified in `index`.

How to do it...

In the following example, we will create a menu that contains an option to exit the application. Create the following text file and save it in your working path with the name `my_menu.tcl`:

```
# Load the TK Package
package require Tk
#Define our interface
wm geometry . 320x240
wm title . "Menu Example"
# Create a menu to exit our application
menu .myMenu
.configure -menu .myMenu
# Add a pull down
set File [menu .myMenu.myfile]
.myMenu add cascade -label File -menu .myMenu.myfile
# Add the Exit entry
$File add command -label Exit -command exit
```

Now launch the program by invoking the following command line command.

`tclsh85 my_menu.tcl`

You should now see the following window:

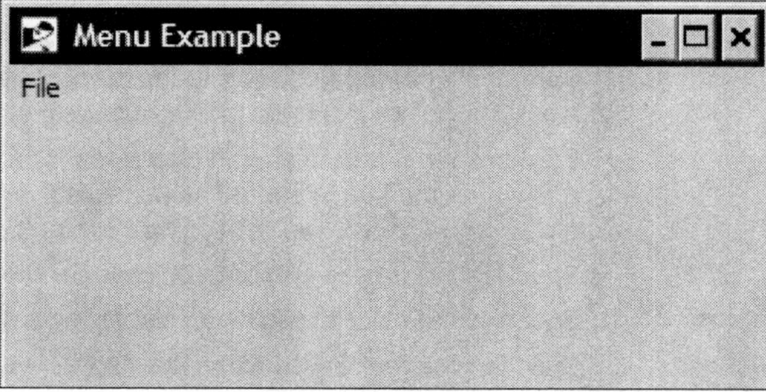

Click on the **File** menu item to display the **Exit** option. Select this option to exit the window.

How it works...

Based on the configuration options provided to the `menu` command we have created a menu with an entry to exit our program.

Adding menu buttons

The `menubutton` command is very similar to the `menu` command. However, as opposed to creating a standard or pop-up menu, it creates a menu consisting of buttons, as the name implies. The syntax is as follows:

```
menubutton name option value …
```

The `menubutton` command accepts one or more `option value` pairs, as detailed in the following table:

Option	Interpretation
`-activebackground`	Specifies the background color to be used when drawing the element. The active background is the color used when the mouse is over the element and when pressing the mouse button will initiate an action.
`-activeforeground`	Specifies the foreground color to be used when drawing the element. The active foreground is the color used when the mouse is over the element and when pressing the mouse button will initiate an action.
`-anchor`	Specifies how the information within the widget is displayed. Acceptable values are `n`, `ne`, `se`, `s`, `sw`, `w`, `nw`, or `center` (default).

Option	Interpretation
-background or -bg	Specifies the background color to be used when drawing the element.
-bitmap	Specifies a bitmap to display in the menu instead of a textual label. This is not available for separator or tearoff items.
-compound	Specifies if the button should display both an image and text and where the image should be displayed. Acceptable values are bottom, center, left, none (default), right, or top.
-cursor	Specifies the mouse cursor to be used for the window.
-disabledforeground	Specifies the color to use when displaying a disabled element.
-font	Specifies the font to use when drawing the element.
-foreground or -fg	Specifies the normal foreground color to be used when drawing the element.
-highlightbackground	Specifies the color to display in the highlight region when the button does not have focus.
-highlightcolor	Specifies the color to display in the highlight region when the button does have focus.
-highlightthickness	Specifies the width of the highlight region (rectangle) to draw around the outside of the button when it has focus.
-image	Specifies an image to display in place of a bitmap or textual label. This is not available for separator or tearoff items.
-justify	Specifies how to display textual information when the button contains multiple lines of text. Acceptable values are left, center, or right.
-padx	Specifies the amount of additional x-space to allot for the button.
-pady	Specifies the amount of additional y-space to allot for the button.
-takefocus	Determines whether or not the window accepts the focus during keyboard traversal.
-direction	Specifies where the pop up menu will be displayed in relation to the button. Acceptable values are above, below, flush, left, and right.
-height	Specifies the height of the menu button. If an image or a bitmap is used, the value is supplied as screen units, if textual then it refers to the number of lines. If not specified the button height is computed based on the contents.
-indicatoron	A Boolean value is provided to determine if a small indicator rectangle is displayed to the right of the button.
-menu	Specifies the pathname of a menu to associate with the button.

Option	Interpretation
-state	Specifies the state of the menu button. Acceptable values are normal, active, or disabled.
-width	Specifies the height of the menu button. If an image or bitmap is used the value is supplied as screen units, if textual, it refers to the number of lines. If not specified, the button height is computed based on the contents.

Creation of the menubutton widget additionally created a new Tcl command of the same name. These commands are accessed using the following syntax:

```
name command arguments
```

The commands are as follows:

Specific commands	Interpretation
name cget option	Returns the current configuration value for the option specified.
name configure option value...	Query or modify the option of the menu.

How to do it...

In the following example, we will create a menu button that contains an option to exit a window. Create the following text file and save it in your working path with the name my_menubutton.tcl:

```
# Load the TK Package
package require Tk

#Define our interface
wm geometry . 320x240
wm title . "Menu Example"

# Create a menubutton to exit our window
menubutton .menu1 -text File -menu .menu1.m -underline 0 -relief
raised

# Add a pull down
menu .menu1.m
.menu1.m add command -label Quit -command exit

# Pack the menubutton
pack .menu1 -anchor nw
```

Now launch the program by invoking the following command line command.

```
tclsh85 my_menubutton.tcl
```

You should now see the following window:

Access your cascading menu and select the **Exit** option to close the window.

How it works...

Based on the configuration options provided to the `menubutton` command, we have created a menu button with a submenu. Selecting the **Quit** entry we can close our program.

Displaying a pop-up menu

A pop-up menu is exactly as the name implies: a menu that appears arbitrarily. It is accessed via a user action (normally a mouse click). The menu is created as normally, but is accessed by binding to an event. The actual display of the menu is accomplished by the `tk_popup` command.

The syntax is as follows:

```
tk_popup name x y
```

How to do it...

In the following example, we will create a menu that contains an option to exit a window. Create the following text file and save it in your working path with the name `my_popup.tcl`:

```
# Load the TK Package
package require Tk

#Define our interface
```

```
wm geometry . 320x240
wm title . "Menu Example"

# Create a menu to exit our window
set File [menu .popup]

# Add the Exit entry
$File add command -label Exit -command exit

# Now we add a label to bind to
label .l -text "Click here to access your menu"
pack .l

# Now bind to the right mouse click
bind .l <3> {tk_popup .popup %X %Y}
```

Now launch the program by invoking the following command line command.

tclsh85 my_popup.tcl

You should now see the following window after you right-click on the label:

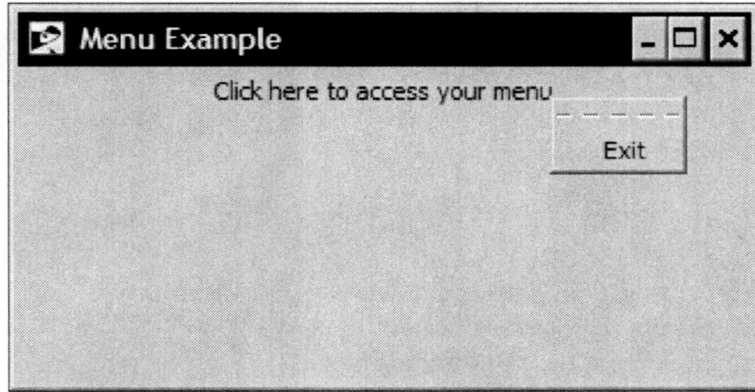

Click on the label to access your pop up menu and select the Exit option to close the window.

How it works...

By binding the right mouse click to the label we have displayed a pop up menu. Bear in mind that specific platform differences may exist for example between Windows and the MacOS X platforms. The `%X` and `%Y` are returned by the mouse click event and the upper-left-hand side corner of the pop up is positioned at this location. To remove the menu from the display without invoking a `menu` command, you simply click on any area of the window.

Data entry application

We will now add a more complex menu to our data entry application. This menu will allow the user to manage the functionality of the application via the menu in the same manner as they would when using the buttons.

How to do it...

In the following example, we will create a menu that contains an option to exit a window. Create the following text file and save it in your working path with the name `address_book.tcl`:

```
# Load the Tk Package
package require Tk

# Main Frame
frame .main -borderwidth 1 -relief solid -padx 10 -pady 10

# Entry Widgets
entry .main.efirst -width 25
entry .main.elast -width 25
entry .main.eaddress -width 50
entry .main.ecity -width 25
entry .main.estate -width 3
entry .main.ezip -width 5
entry .main.ephone -width 25

# Label Widgets
label .main.first -text "First Name"
label .main.last -text "Last Name"
label .main.address -text "Address"
label .main.city -text "City"
label .main.state -text "ST"
label .main.zip -text "Zip"
label .main.phone -text "Phone"
label .main.photo -text "Photo" -width 15

# Frame for Photo Widget
frame .main.picture -width 120 -height 160 -borderwidth 3 -background
black

# Button Widgets
button .main.previous -text "Previous" -width 15
button .main.next -text "Next" -width 15
button .main.add -text "Add" -width 15
button .main.save -text "Save" -width 15
button .main.delete -text "Delete" -width 15
```

```
button .main.exit -text "Exit" -width 15 -command exit

# Pack Command
pack .main

# Grid command
grid configure .main.efirst -row 0 -column 0 -sticky nw
grid configure .main.elast -row 0 -column 1 -columnspan 2 -sticky nw
grid configure .main.picture -row 0 -column 3 -rowspan 7 -sticky nw
grid configure .main.first -row 1 -column 0 -sticky nw
grid configure .main.last -row 1 -column 1 -columnspan 2 -sticky nw
grid configure .main.eaddress -row 2 -column 0 -columnspan 3 -sticky
nw
grid configure .main.address -row 3 -column 0 -columnspan 3 -sticky nw
grid configure .main.ecity -row 4 -column 0 -sticky nw
grid configure .main.estate -row 4 -column 1 -sticky nw
grid configure .main.ezip -row 4 -column 2 -sticky nw
grid configure .main.city -row 5 -column 0 -sticky nw
grid configure .main.state -row 5 -column 1 -sticky nw
grid configure .main.zip -row 5 -column 2 -sticky nw
grid configure .main.ephone -row 6 -column 0 -columnspan 2 -sticky nw
grid configure .main.phone -row 7 -column 0 -columnspan 2 -sticky nw
grid configure .main.photo -row 7 -column 3 -sticky nw
grid configure .main.previous -row 8 -column 0 -sticky ne
grid configure .main.next -row 8 -column 2 -sticky nw
grid configure .main.add -row 9 -column 0 -sticky ne
grid configure .main.save -row 9 -column 1 -sticky nw
grid configure .main.delete -row 9 -column 2 -sticky nw
grid configure .main.exit -row 9 -column 3 -sticky nw

# Menu Creation
menu .menubar
. configure -menu .menubar

# Add the first item
set File [menu .menubar.myfile]
.menubar add cascade -label File -menu .menubar.myfile

# Add entries
$File add command -label "Add Record" -command addRecord
$File add command -label "Save Record" -command saveRecord
$File add command -label "Delete Record" -command deleteRecord
$File add separator
$File add command -label "Quit" -command exit

set Edit [menu .menubar.myedit]
.menubar add cascade -label Edit -menu .menubar.myedit

$Edit add command -label "Find" -command findRecord
```

Now launch the program by invoking the following command line.

```
tclsh85 address_book.tcl
```

You should now see the following window:

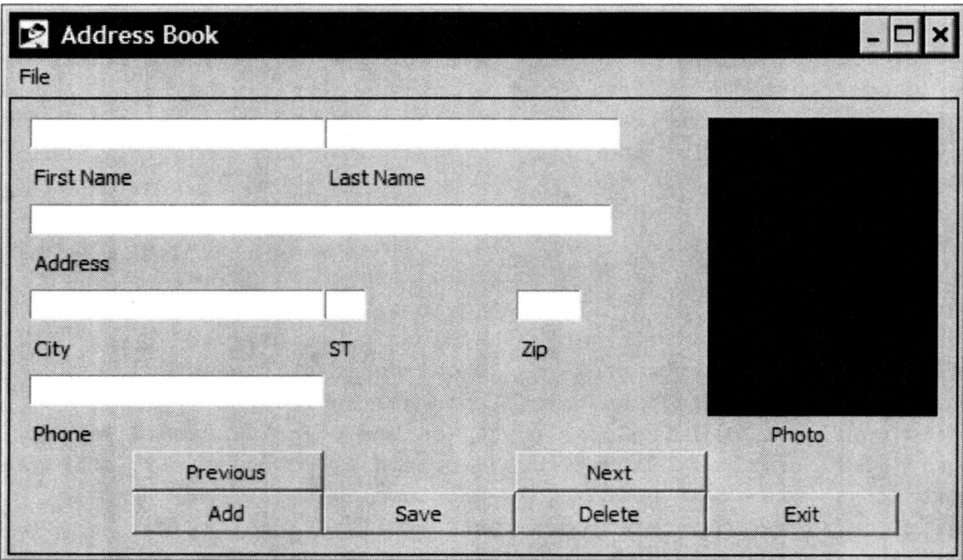

How it works...

We have now added a menu to our Address Book application. The entries are bound in such a manner that they will mirror the functionality of the buttons. At this point, there are no associated commands, as they will be written in the following chapter, when we complete the application.

13
Creating the Address Book Application

In this chapter, we will cover:

- Creating the address book application
- Adding a record
- Navigating records
- Deleting a record
- Finding a record
- Full listing

Introduction

In the Address Book application, we will bring together everything covered within the previous chapters. This will include not only the Tcl commands and Tk widgets, but also the creation of global variables and calling Tcl procedures. We will leverage the flexibility of the `dict` command combined with the `list` command to read and write our data to disk in a manner similar to a database.

I have also added comments to clarify understanding of various sections. Although these comments are not necessary for the program to operate, you should add them to aid you in the event of any issues you might encounter.

Please note that I have intentionally used step-by-step methodology to complete several items, as opposed to a control construct methodology, to more clearly illustrate sections. For example, rather that storing the widgets in a list and creating them with a while statement, I have created them one by one.

To complete the following example, open the text editor of your choice and enter the text as directed. Then save the file in your path with the name `address_book.tcl`. Also, note that I have left code that will write messages to the console, based on specific actions to illustrate using the console output to debug your programs as you create them.

Creating the Address Book application

As with any Tcl/Tk application, the manner in which the script is created determines the behavior. This is especially apparent when interacting with global variables. The global variables for our application are defined in the main body of the script to allow them to be accessed by the procedures. For the sake of formatting, I have used line continuation characters, "\" that may not be required in your text editor.

How to do it...

First, we will start by creating the graphical user interface. Enter the following into the `address_book` Tcl file:

```
# Load the Tk Package
package require Tk

# Configure the Window
wm title . "Address Book"

# Main Frame
frame .main -borderwidth 1 -relief solid -padx 10 -pady 10

# Entry Widgets
entry.main.efirst -width 25
entry .main.elast -width 25
entry .main.eaddress -width 50
entry .main.ecity -width 25
entry .main.estate -width 3
entry .main.ezip -width 5
entry .main.ephone -width 25

# Label Widgets
label .main.first -text "First Name"
label .main.last -text "Last Name"
label .main.address -text "Address"
label .main.city -text "City"
label .main.state -text "ST"
label .main.zip -text "Zip"
label .main.phone -text "Phone"
label .main.photo -text "Click to Update" -width 15

# Label for Photo Widget
```

```
label .main.picture -background black

# Button Widgets
button .main.previous -text "Previous" -width 15 -command
previousRecord
button .main.next -text "Next" -width 15 -command nextRecord
button .main.add -text "Add" -width 15 -command addRecord
button .main.save -text "Save" -width 15 -command saveRecord
button .main.delete -text "Delete" -width 15 -command deleteRecord
button .main.exit -text "Exit" -width 15 -command exit

# Pack command
pack .main

# Grid command
grid .main.efirst -row 0 -column 0 -sticky nw
grid .main.elast -row 0 -column 1 -columnspan 2 -sticky nw
grid .main.picture -row 0 -column 3 -rowspan 7 -sticky news
grid .main.first -row 1 -column 0 -sticky nw
grid .main.last -row 1 -column 1 -columnspan 2 -sticky nw
grid .main.eaddress -row 2 -column 0 -columnspan 3 -sticky nw
grid .main.address -row 3 -column 0 -columnspan 3 -sticky nw
grid .main.ecity -row 4 -column 0 -sticky nw
grid .main.estate -row 4 -column 1 -sticky nw
grid .main.ezip -row 4 -column 2 -sticky nw
grid .main.city -row 5 -column 0 -sticky nw
grid .main.state -row 5 -column 1 -sticky nw
grid .main.zip -row 5 -column 2 -sticky nw
grid .main.ephone -row 6 -column 0 -columnspan 2 -sticky nw
grid .main.phone -row 7 -column 0 -columnspan 2 -sticky nw
grid .main.photo -row 7 -column 3 -sticky nw
grid .main.previous -row 8 -column 0 -sticky ne
grid .main.next -row 8 -column 2 -sticky nw
grid .main.add -row 9 -column 0 -sticky ne
grid .main.save -row 9 -column 1 -sticky nw
grid .main.delete -row 9 -column 2 -sticky nw
grid .main.exit -row 9 -column 3 -sticky nw

# Menu Creation
menu .menubar
. configure -menu .menubar

# Add the first item
set File [menu .menubar.myfile]
.menubar add cascade -label File -menu .menubar.myfile

# Add entries
$File add command -label "Add Record" -command addRecord
```

```
$File add command -label "Save Record" -command saveRecord
$File add command -label "Delete Record" -command deleteRecord
$File add separator
$File add command -label "Quit" -command exit

# Add the second item
set Edit [menu .menubar.myedit]
.menubar add cascade -label Edit -menu .menubar.myedit

# Add entry
$Edit add command -label "Find" -command findRecord

# Bind the mouse click to the picture label
bind .main.picture <B1-ButtonRelease> getPicture

# Text file containing stored records
global addressFile
# Dictionary used for working with records
global addressInfo
# Current Record
global currentRecord
# Record Count
global recordCount
# Image File location
global pictureFile

# Initialization of the address file
set addressFile "address.txt"

# Create the dictionary from the file on disk
# if it exists and contains entries

if { [file exists $addressFile]} {
 # If the file exists check that it has contents
 # Since we are managing the file through the application we can
assume
 # for the sake of our application that it is in the correct format

  if { [file size $addressFile] > 0 } {
    set fp [open $addressFile r+]
    gets $fp data

    while {$data >0} {
      set data2 [split $data ","]

      set recno [lindex $data2 0]

      dict set addressInfo $recno ID [lindex $data2 0]
      dict set addressInfo $recno FNAME [lindex $data2 1]
      dict set addressInfo $recno LNAME [lindex $data2 2]
      dict set addressInfo $recno ADDRESS [lindex $data2 3]
      dict set addressInfo $recno CITY [lindex $data2 4]
```

```
        dict set addressInfo $recno STATE [lindex $data2 5]
        dict set addressInfo $recno ZIP [lindex $data2 6]
        dict set addressInfo $recno PHONE [lindex $data2 7]
        dict set addressInfo $recno PHOTO [lindex $data2 8]
        # Open the file
        set pictureFile [dict get $addressInfo $recno PHOTO]
        # Read the data using the gets
        gets $fp data
      }
      close $fp
      set recordCount [dict size $addressInfo]
      set currentRecord 1
      # Load the first record
      loadRecord
       } else {
        set myTitle "Missing Records"
        set myMessage \ "No records exist, please add an entry and click
                        save"
        tk_messageBox -message $myMessage \
        -title $myTitle \
        -type ok \
        -icon warning
        set currentRecord 0
        set recordCount 0
        set pictureFile ""
      }
  } else {
    set myTitle "Missing configuration file"
    set myMessage \ "No address file exists, please add an entry and
click save."
    tk_messageBox -message $myMessage \
      -title myTitle \
      -icon warning
      set currentRecord 0
      set recordCount 0
      set pictureFile ""
  }
```

How it works...

First, we created our interface using a set of Tk widgets. After the creation of the interface we checked for the existence of a data file. If no file existed, we notified the end user. If the file existed, we checked its contents. If no contents existed, we notified the end user. If the file existed and it had entries, we opened the file. After opening the file we configured it for reading line-by-line and then read the data into our dictionary. Note that at this time, if you run the program, it will fail due to the fact that there are missing procedures to load the records and display the photos. These procedures are contained in the following sections.

Adding a record

Now that we have an interface it would be nice to have records. To accomplish this, we need to give the user the ability to add a record including a photo if desired. This will require that we set up our variables to support adding a record, clear the interface, associate a picture to the entry and then save the record when the user is complete as well as a procedure to load the record for display.

How to do it...

In the address book file, enter the following text at the location defined in our main page for procedures as defined within the comments:

```
proc addRecord {} {
  global currentRecord
  global recordCount
  global addressInfo
  global pictureFile
  # Clear current entries
  clearRecord
  set pictureFile ""
  set currentRecord [expr $recordCount +1]
}
# Clear any contents from the entry widgets
proc clearRecord {} {
  .main.efirst delete 0 end
  .main.elast delete 0 end
  .main.eaddress delete 0 end
  .main.ecity delete 0 end
  .main.estate delete 0 end
  .main.ezip delete 0 end
  .main.ephone delete 0 end
  .main.picture configure -image ""
```

```
}
proc getPicture {} {
  global currentRecord
  global addressInfo
  global pictureFile

  set types {
    {{GIF} {.gif}  }
    {{PPM} {.ppm}  }
    {{All Files} *  }
  }

  set filename [tk_getOpenFile -filetypes $types]

  if {$filename != ""} {
    # Now that we have the path to the desired picture
    # we copy it to the working directory

    # Get the destination filename
    # by splitting the fullpath into
    # elements and retrieving the last
    set listFile [file split $filename]
    set listCount [llength $listFile]
    set listIndex [expr $listCount - 1]

    set pictureFile [lindex $listFile $listIndex]

    # If the pictureFile already exists within the
    # working directory we do not copy it again
    if { [file exists $pictureFile] == 0 } {
      # Copy the image to the current directory
      if {[catch {file copy -force "$filename" $pictureFile} sError]}
        {
          tk_messageBox -message "File Copy Error $filename to
            $pictureFile"
      }
    }

    # Update the dictionary entry

    dict set addressInfo $currentRecord PHOTO $pictureFile

    # Update the image onscreen
    image create photo newPicture -file $pictureFile
    .main.picture configure -image newPicture
  }
}
proc saveRecord {} {
```

```
  global currentRecord
  global recordCount
  global addressFile
  global addressInfo
  global pictureFile

  # No Records Exist
  if { $currentRecord == 0 } {
    incr currentRecord
    incr recordCount
  }

  dict set addressInfo $currentRecord ID "$currentRecord"
  dict set addressInfo $currentRecord FNAME "[.main.efirst get]"
  dict set addressInfo $currentRecord LNAME "[.main.elast get]"
  dict set addressInfo $currentRecord ADDRESS "[.main.eaddress get]"
  dict set addressInfo $currentRecord CITY "[.main.ecity get]"
  dict set addressInfo $currentRecord STATE "[.main.estate get]"
  dict set addressInfo $currentRecord ZIP "[.main.ezip get]"
  dict set addressInfo $currentRecord PHONE "[.main.ephone get]"
  dict set addressInfo $currentRecord PHOTO "$pictureFile"

  # Write the records to the file

  set fp [open $addressFile w+]

  dict for {id info} $addressInfo {
    dict with info {
      # Create an entry for the file
     set data "$ID,$FNAME,$LNAME,$ADDRESS,$CITY,$STATE,$ZIP, \
     $PHONE,$PHOTO\n"
      # Write the entry to the file
       puts -nonewline $fp $data
     }
   }
  set recordCount [dict size $addressInfo]
  # Close the file
  close $fp
}
# This procedure is used to load and display a record
# from the dictionary
proc loadRecord { } {
  global currentRecord
  global addressInfo

  .main.efirst insert 0 [dict get $addressInfo $currentRecord FNAME]
  .main.elast insert 0 [dict get $addressInfo $currentRecord LNAME]
```

```
  .main.eaddress insert 0 [dict get $addressInfo $currentRecord \
ADDRESS]
  .main.ecity insert 0 [dict get $addressInfo $currentRecord CITY]
  .main.estate insert 0 [dict get $addressInfo $currentRecord STATE]
  .main.ezip insert 0 [dict get $addressInfo $currentRecord ZIP]
  .main.ephone insert 0 [dict get $addressInfo $currentRecord PHONE]

  # Load the photo
  if {[dict get $addressInfo $currentRecord PHOTO] > 0} {
    set pictureFile [dict get $addressInfo $currentRecord PHOTO]
    image create photo addressPhoto -file $pictureFile
    .main.picture configure -image addressPhoto
  }
}
```

How it works...

First, we configured our counters (record and total) and then cleared the screen. This is in preparation for the user to add some data. Once the user selects the **Save** button, we add the contents of the entry widgets to the dictionary and write them to the data file for future use. Then we display the record. Note that if the user simply changes a record and clicks on **Save**, he will be performing an edit of the existing record.

Navigating records

Now that we can add records, we need a means to scroll through them. This is where the **Next** and **Previous** command buttons come into play. To accomplish this, we will create two procedures.

How to do it...

In the address book file, enter the following text at the location defined in our main page for procedures, as defined within the comments after the previous section's procedures.

```
proc nextRecord {} {
  global currentRecord
  global recordCount

  if {$currentRecord < $recordCount} {
    # Clear current entries
    clearRecord
    incr currentRecord
    loadRecord
  }
```

```
  }

  proc previousRecord {} {
    global currentRecord
    global recordCount

    if {$currentRecord > 1} {
      # Clear current entries
      clearRecord

      set currentRecord [expr $currentRecord - 1]
      loadRecord
    }
  }
```

How it works...

These procedures simply increment or decrement the record counter if it is within the range of the number of records and then calls our previously created procedure to load the record.

Deleting a record

Adding records is complete as is navigating between them. So now we need the ability to remove records from both the active dictionary and the data file. This is accomplished with a single procedure. Care must be taken to address the fact that a user may click on **Delete** when no records exist and to handle the condition where the user has deleted all records.

How to do it...

In the address book file, enter the following text at the location defined in our main page for procedures, as defined within the comments after the previous section's procedures.

```
  proc deleteRecord {} {
    global addressFile
    global addressInfo
    global currentRecord
    global recordCount

    if {$recordCount > 0} {
      set myTitle "Confirm Request"
      set myMessage "Select OK to delete the current record"
      set response [tk_messageBox -message $myMessage \
        -title myTitle \
        -type okcancel \
        -icon warning]

      if {$response == "ok"} {
```

```
puts "DELETE COUNT: $recordCount CURRENT: $currentRecord"
set tempDict [dict remove $addressInfo $currentRecord]

clearRecord

puts "IN DELETE"
set fp [open $addressFile w+]
puts "DELETE FILE ID: $fp"

set recnum 0

dict for {id info} $tempDict {

  dict with info {
    incr recnum
    # Create an entry for the file
    set data "$recnum,$FNAME,$LNAME,$ADDRESS,$CITY, \
    $STATE,$ZIP, $PHONE,$PHOTO\n"
    puts "---"
    puts "NEW DATA: $data"
    # Write the entry to the file
     puts -nonewline $fp $data
  }
}
flush $fp
close $fp

puts "POST DELETE FILE WRITE - READING IN NEW FILE"

# Clean up the dictionary files
unset addressInfo
unset tempDict

# If we deleted the last record this avoid trying to read in an
  empty file
if {[file size $addressFile] > 0} {
  set fp [open $addressFile r+]
  fconfigure $fp -buffering line
  gets $fp data

  set recno 0
  while {$data > 0} {
    puts "DATA ADDED TO DICT: $data TO RECNO: $recno"
    set data2 [split $data ","]

    incr recno

    dict set addressInfo $recno ID [lindex $data2 0]
    dict set addressInfo $recno FNAME [lindex $data2 1]
    dict set addressInfo $recno LNAME [lindex $data2 2]
    dict set addressInfo $recno ADDRESS [lindex $data2 3]
    dict set addressInfo $recno CITY [lindex $data2 4]
```

```
            dict set addressInfo $recno STATE [lindex $data2 5]
            dict set addressInfo $recno ZIP [lindex $data2 6]
            dict set addressInfo $recno PHONE [lindex $data2 7]
            dict set addressInfo $recno PHOTO [lindex $data2 8]
            set pictureFile [dict get $addressInfo $recno PHOTO]
            gets $fp data
            }
          set recordCount [dict size $addressInfo]
          puts "NEW addressInfo recordCount $recordCount\n\n"
          set currentRecord 1
          # Load the first record
          loadRecord
        } else {
          set myTitle "Missing Records"
          set myMessage \ "No records exist, please add an entry and
              click save"
          tk_messageBox -message $myMessage \
          -title $myTitle \
          -type ok \
          -icon warning
          set currentRecord 0
          set recordCount 0
          set pictureFile ""
        }
      }
    }
  }
```

How it works...

First we check to ensure that for a record to be deleted, it exists. This addresses the user selecting delete when there are no records or deleting all records. Once we are convinced that we can proceed, we remove the entry from the dictionary using the `dict remove` command to create a temporary dictionary containing only the record set desired, write the data to file, read it back into our global dictionary, and display the record.

Finding a record

Locating a record is a common procedure in most data-driven applications. In our application, we have limited this to locating the first occurrence by last name. To accomplish this, we will create a new `toplevel` window to request input and trigger procedures that interact with our main window.

How to do it...

In the address book file, enter the following text at the location defined in our main page for procedures, as defined within the comments after the previous section's procedures.

```
proc findRecord { } {
    set strLast ""
    toplevel .find
    frame .find.f -borderwidth 1 -relief solid -padx 10 -pady 10
    entry .find.f.e -borderwidth 5 -relief solid
    button .find.f.ok -text "Find" -command {set strLast [.find.f.e \
            get]; lookup $strLast}
    button .find.f.cancel -text "Cancel" -command {destroy .find}
    pack .find.f
    grid .find.f.e -row 0 -column 0 -columnspan 2 -sticky news
    grid .find.f.ok -row 1 -column 0 -sticky news
    grid .find.f.cancel -row 1 -column 1 -sticky news
}

proc lookup {strLast} {
    global addressInfo
    global currentRecord

    puts "LOOKING for $strLast"

    dict for {id info} $addressInfo {
           dict with info {
                  if {"$strLast" == "$LNAME"} {
                         puts "NAME: $LNAME"
                         puts "FOUND ONE"
                         set currentRecord "$ID"
                         clearRecord
                         loadRecord
                  }
           }
    }
}
```

How it works...

After creating and displaying a new top level window, we perform a string comparison on the global dictionary to find the first matching instance. The top level window will remain visible until the **Cancel** button is clicked and the user can complete numerous searches.

Full listing

This section contains a full listing of the address book application, as it should look in your program. This is a basic data entry application that highlights many of the functionalities of the Tcl/Tk language. At this point, you may wish to sort the dictionary to provide an alphabetical listing of the data, implement multiple field search capability, and toggle the state of the buttons and menu entries to limit the user's abilities in a logical manner or anything else you might want to add.

It's all there in Tcl/Tk. The only limit is your imagination.

```
# Source the Tk Package
package require Tk

#Configure the Window
wm title . "Address Book"

# Main Frame
frame .main -borderwidth 1 -relief solid -padx 10 -pady 10

# Entry Widgets
entry .main.efirst -width 25
entry .main.elast -width 25
entry .main.eaddress -width 50
entry .main.ecity -width 25
entry .main.estate -width 3
entry .main.ezip -width 5
entry .main.ephone -width 25

# Label Widgets
label .main.first -text "First Name"
label .main.last -text "Last Name"
label .main.address -text "Address"
label .main.city -text "City"
label .main.state -text "ST"
label .main.zip -text "Zip"
label .main.phone -text "Phone"
label .main.photo -text "Click to Update" -width 15

# Label for Photo Widget
label .main.picture -background black
```

```
# -width 15 -height 10

# Button Widgets
button .main.previous -text "Previous" -width 15 -command
previousRecord
button .main.next -text "Next" -width 15 -command nextRecord
button .main.add -text "Add" -width 15 -command addRecord
button .main.save -text "Save" -width 15 -command saveRecord
button .main.delete -text "Delete" -width 15 -command deleteRecord
button .main.exit -text "Exit" -width 15 -command exit

# Pack command
pack .main

# Grid command
grid .main.efirst -row 0 -column 0 -sticky nw
grid .main.elast -row 0 -column 1 -columnspan 2 -sticky nw
grid .main.picture -row 0 -column 3 -rowspan 7 -sticky news
grid .main.first -row 1 -column 0 -sticky nw
grid .main.last -row 1 -column 1 -columnspan 2 -sticky nw
grid .main.eaddress -row 2 -column 0 -columnspan 3 -sticky nw
grid .main.address -row 3 -column 0 -columnspan 3 -sticky nw
grid .main.ecity -row 4 -column 0 -sticky nw
grid .main.estate -row 4 -column 1 -sticky nw
grid .main.ezip -row 4 -column 2 -sticky nw
grid .main.city -row 5 -column 0 -sticky nw
grid .main.state -row 5 -column 1 -sticky nw
grid .main.zip -row 5 -column 2 -sticky nw
grid .main.ephone -row 6 -column 0 -columnspan 2 -sticky nw
grid .main.phone -row 7 -column 0 -columnspan 2 -sticky nw
grid .main.photo -row 7 -column 3 -sticky nw
grid .main.previous -row 8 -column 0 -sticky ne
grid .main.next -row 8 -column 2 -sticky nw
grid .main.add -row 9 -column 0 -sticky ne
grid .main.save -row 9 -column 1 -sticky nw
grid .main.delete -row 9 -column 2 -sticky nw
grid .main.exit -row 9 -column 3 -sticky nw

# Menu Creation
menu .menubar
.configure -menu .menubar

# Add the first item
set File [menu .menubar.myfile]
.menubar add cascade -label File -menu .menubar.myfile

# Add entries
$File add command -label "Add Record" -command addRecord
```

```
$File add command -label "Save Record" -command saveRecord
$File add command -label "Delete Record" -command deleteRecord
$File add separator
$File add command -label "Quit" -command exit

set Edit [menu .menubar.myedit]
.menubar add cascade -label Edit -menu .menubar.myedit

$Edit add command -label "Find" -command findRecord

# Bind the mouse click to the picture label
bind .main.picture <B1-ButtonRelease> getPicture

# Global Variables
# Text file containing stored records
global addressFile
# Dictionary used for working with records
global addressInfo
# Current Record
global currentRecord
# Record Count
global recordCount
# Image File location
global pictureFile

set addressFile "address.txt"

##########################################
#    Procedures    #
##########################################

proc findRecord { } {

  set strLast ""

  toplevel .find
  frame .find.f -borderwidth 1 -relief solid -padx 10 -pady 10
  entry .find.f.e -borderwidth 5 -relief solid
  button .find.f.ok -text "Find" -command {set strLast [.find.f.e \
get]; lookup $strLast}
  button .find.f.cancel -text "Cancel" -command {destroy .find}

  pack .find.f
  grid .find.f.e -row 0 -column 0 -columnspan 2 -sticky news
  grid .find.f.ok -row 1 -column 0 -sticky news
  grid .find.f.cancel -row 1 -column 1 -sticky news
}

proc lookup {strLast} {
  global addressInfo
  global currentRecord
```

```
  puts "LOOKING for $strLast"
  dict for {id info} $addressInfo {
    dict with info {
       if {"$strLast" == "$LNAME"} {
        puts "NAME: $LNAME"
        puts "FOUND ONE"
        set currentRecord "$ID"
        clearRecord
        loadRecord
      }
    }
  }
}
# This procedure is used to load and display a record
# from the dictionary
proc loadRecord { } {
  global currentRecord
  global addressInfo
  .main.efirst insert 0 [dict get $addressInfo $currentRecord FNAME]
  .main.elast insert 0 [dict get $addressInfo $currentRecord LNAME]
  .main.eaddress insert 0 [dict get $addressInfo $currentRecord
   ADDRESS]
  .main.ecity insert 0 [dict get $addressInfo $currentRecord CITY]
  .main.estate insert 0 [dict get $addressInfo $currentRecord STATE]
  .main.ezip insert 0 [dict get $addressInfo $currentRecord ZIP]
  .main.ephone insert 0 [dict get $addressInfo $currentRecord PHONE]

  # Load the photo
  if {[dict get $addressInfo $currentRecord PHOTO] > 0} {
    set pictureFile [dict get $addressInfo $currentRecord PHOTO]
    image create photo addressPhoto -file $pictureFile
    .main.picture configure -image addressPhoto
  }
}
proc clearRecord {} {
  .main.efirst delete 0 end
  .main.elast delete 0 end
  .main.eaddress delete 0 end
  .main.ecity delete 0 end
  .main.estate delete 0 end
  .main.ezip delete 0 end
  .main.ephone delete 0 end
```

```
    .main.picture configure -image ""
  }
  proc addRecord {} {
    global currentRecord
    global recordCount
    global addressInfo
    global pictureFile
    # Clear current entries
    clearRecord
    set pictureFile ""
    set currentRecord [expr $recordCount +1]
  }
  proc nextRecord {} {
    global currentRecord
    global recordCount

    if { $currentRecord < $recordCount } {
      # Clear current entries
      clearRecord
      incr currentRecord
      loadRecord
    }
  }
  proc previousRecord {} {
    global currentRecord
    global recordCount
    if { $currentRecord > 1 } {
      # Clear current entries
      clearRecord

      set currentRecord [expr $currentRecord - 1]
      loadRecord
    }
  }
  proc saveRecord {} {
    global currentRecord
    global recordCount
    global addressFile
    global addressInfo
    global pictureFile
    # No Records Exist
    if {$currentRecord == 0} {
      incr currentRecord
```

```
    incr recordCount
  }
  dict set addressInfo $currentRecord ID "$currentRecord"
  dict set addressInfo $currentRecord FNAME "[.main.efirst get]"
  dict set addressInfo $currentRecord LNAME "[.main.elast get]"
  dict set addressInfo $currentRecord ADDRESS "[.main.eaddress get]"
  dict set addressInfo $currentRecord CITY "[.main.ecity get]"
  dict set addressInfo $currentRecord STATE "[.main.estate get]"
  dict set addressInfo $currentRecord ZIP "[.main.ezip get]"
  dict set addressInfo $currentRecord PHONE "[.main.ephone get]"
  dict set addressInfo $currentRecord PHOTO "$pictureFile"
  # Write the records to the file
  set fp [open $addressFile w+]
  dict for {id info} $addressInfo {
    dict with info {
      # Create an entry for the file
       set data "$ID,$FNAME,$LNAME,$ADDRESS,$CITY,$STATE,$ZIP, \
$PHONE,$PHOTO\n"
      # Write the entry to the file
       puts -nonewline $fp $data
     }
   }
  set recordCount [dict size $addressInfo]
  # Close the file
  close $fp
}
proc deleteRecord {} {
  global addressFile
  global addressInfo
  global currentRecord
  global recordCount
  if {$recordCount > 0} {
    set myTitle "Confirm Request"
    set myMessage "Select OK to delete the current record"
    set response [tk_messageBox -message $myMessage \
      -title myTitle \
      -type okcancel \
      -icon warning]
    if {$response == "ok"} {
      puts "DELETE COUNT: $recordCount CURRENT: $currentRecord"
      set tempDict [dict remove $addressInfo $currentRecord]
```

```
clearRecord
puts "IN DELETE"
set fp [open $addressFile w+]
puts "DELETE FILE ID: $fp"
set recnum 0

dict for {id info} $tempDict {
  dict with info {
    incr recnum
    # Create an entry for the file
   set data "$recnum,$FNAME,$LNAME,$ADDRESS,$CITY, \
   $STATE, $ZIP,$PHONE,$PHOTO\n"
    puts "---"
    puts "NEW DATA: $data"
    # Write the entry to the file
     puts -nonewline $fp $data
  }
}
flush $fp
close $fp
puts "POST DELETE FILE WRITE - READING IN NEW FILE"
# Clean up the dictionary files
unset addressInfo
unset tempDict
# If we deleted the last record this avoids trying to read in an
  empty file
if {[file size $addressFile] > 0} {
  set fp [open $addressFile r+]
  fconfigure $fp -buffering line
  gets $fp data
  set recno 0
  while { $data > 0 } {
    puts "DATA ADDED TO DICT: $data TO RECNO: $recno"
    set data2 [split $data ","]
    incr recno
    dict set addressInfo $recno ID [lindex $data2 0]
    dict set addressInfo $recno FNAME [lindex $data2 1]
    dict set addressInfo $recno LNAME [lindex $data2 2]
    dict set addressInfo $recno ADDRESS [lindex $data2 3]
    dict set addressInfo $recno CITY [lindex $data2 4]
    dict set addressInfo $recno STATE [lindex $data2 5]
```

```
            dict set addressInfo $recno ZIP [lindex $data2 6]
            dict set addressInfo $recno PHONE [lindex $data2 7]
            dict set addressInfo $recno PHOTO [lindex $data2 8]
            set pictureFile [dict get $addressInfo $recno PHOTO]
            gets $fp data
            }
          set recordCount [dict size $addressInfo]
          puts "NEW addressInfo recordCount $recordCount\n\n"
          set currentRecord 1
          # Load the first record
          loadRecord
        } else {
          set myTitle "Missing Records"
          set myMessage "No records exist, please add an entry and click
          save"
          tk_messageBox -message $myMessage \
          -title $myTitle \
          -type ok \
          -icon warning
          set currentRecord 0
          set recordCount 0
          set pictureFile ""
        }
      }
    }
  }
proc getPicture {} {
  global currentRecord
  global addressInfo
  global pictureFile
  set types {
    {{GIF} {.gif}  }
    {{PPM} {.ppm}  }
    {{All Files} *  }
  }
  set filename [tk_getOpenFile -filetypes $types]
  if {$filename != ""} {
    # Now that we have the path to the desired picture
    # we copy it to the working directory
    # Get the destination filename
    # by splitting the fullpath into
```

```
    # elements and retrieving the last
    set listFile [file split $filename]
    set listCount [llength $listFile]
    set listIndex [expr $listCount - 1]

    set pictureFile [lindex $listFile $listIndex]

    # If the pictureFile already exists within the
    # working directory we do not copy it again
    if { [file exists $pictureFile] == 0 } {
      # Copy the image to the current directory
      if {[catch {file copy -force "$filename" $pictureFile} sError]}
        {
        tk_messageBox -message "File Copy Error $filename to
        $pictureFile"
      }
    }

    # Update the dictionary entry
    dict set addressInfo $currentRecord PHOTO $pictureFile
    # Update the image onscreen
    image create photo newPicture -file $pictureFile
    .main.picture configure -image newPicture
  }
}
#############################################
# END OF PROCEDURES
#############################################
# Create the dictionary from the file on disk
# if it exists and contains entries
if { [file exists $addressFile]} {
 # If the file exists check that it has contents
 # Since we are managing the file through the application we can
assume
 # for the sake of our application that it is in the correct format
  if { [file size $addressFile] > 0 } {
    set fp [open $addressFile r+]
    gets $fp data
    while {$data >0} {
      set data2 [split $data ","]
      set recno [lindex $data2 0]
      dict set addressInfo $recno ID [lindex $data2 0]
```

```
      dict set addressInfo $recno FNAME [lindex $data2 1]
      dict set addressInfo $recno LNAME [lindex $data2 2]
      dict set addressInfo $recno ADDRESS [lindex $data2 3]
      dict set addressInfo $recno CITY [lindex $data2 4]
      dict set addressInfo $recno STATE [lindex $data2 5]
      dict set addressInfo $recno ZIP [lindex $data2 6]
      dict set addressInfo $recno PHONE [lindex $data2 7]
      dict set addressInfo $recno PHOTO [lindex $data2 8]
      # Open the file
      set pictureFile [dict get $addressInfo $recno PHOTO]
      # Read the data using the gets
 gets $fp data
    }
    close $fp
    set recordCount [dict size $addressInfo]
    set currentRecord 1
    # Load the first record
    loadRecord
     } else {
      set myTitle "Missing Records"
      set myMessage "No records exist, please add an entry and click
        save"
      tk_messageBox -message $myMessage \
      -title $myTitle \
      -type ok \
      -icon warning
      set currentRecord 0
      set recordCount 0
      set pictureFile ""
    }
} else {
  set myTitle "Missing configuration file"
  set myMessage "No address file exists, please add an entry and click
    save."
  tk_messageBox -message $myMessage \
    -title myTitle \
    -icon warning
    set currentRecord 0
    set recordCount 0
    set pictureFile ""
}
```

Index

D

G

I

J

L

M

N

O

P

T

U

V

W

Thank you for buying
Tcl/Tk 8.5 Programming Cookbook

About Packt Publishing

Packt, pronounced 'packed', published its first book "*Mastering phpMyAdmin for Effective MySQL Management*" in April 2004 and subsequently continued to specialize in publishing highly focused books on specific technologies and solutions.

Our books and publications share the experiences of your fellow IT professionals in adapting and customizing today's systems, applications, and frameworks. Our solution based books give you the knowledge and power to customize the software and technologies you're using to get the job done. Packt books are more specific and less general than the IT books you have seen in the past. Our unique business model allows us to bring you more focused information, giving you more of what you need to know, and less of what you don't.

Packt is a modern, yet unique publishing company, which focuses on producing quality, cutting-edge books for communities of developers, administrators, and newbies alike. For more information, please visit our website: `www.packtpub.com`.

About Packt Open Source

In 2010, Packt launched two new brands, Packt Open Source and Packt Enterprise, in order to continue its focus on specialization. This book is part of the Packt Open Source brand, home to books published on software built around Open Source licences, and offering information to anybody from advanced developers to budding web designers. The Open Source brand also runs Packt's Open Source Royalty Scheme, by which Packt gives a royalty to each Open Source project about whose software a book is sold.

Writing for Packt

We welcome all inquiries from people who are interested in authoring. Book proposals should be sent to author@packtpub.com. If your book idea is still at an early stage and you would like to discuss it first before writing a formal book proposal, contact us; one of our commissioning editors will get in touch with you.

We're not just looking for published authors; if you have strong technical skills but no writing experience, our experienced editors can help you develop a writing career, or simply get some additional reward for your expertise.

Tcl 8.5 Network Programming

ISBN: 978-1-849510-96-7 Paperback: 588 pages

Build network-aware applications using Tcl, a powerful dynamic programming language

1. Develop network-aware applications with Tcl
2. Implement the most important network protocols in Tcl
3. Packed with hands-on-examples, case studies, and clear explanations for better understanding

---

wxPython 2.8 Application Development Cookbook

ISBN: 978-1-84951-178-0 Paperback: 308 pages

Over 80 practical recipes for developing feature-rich applications using wxPython

1. Develop flexible applications in wxPython.
2. Create interface translatable applications that will run on Windows, Macintosh OSX, Linux, and other UNIX like environments.
3. Learn basic and advanced user interface controls.
4. Packed with practical, hands-on cookbook recipes and plenty of example code, illustrating the techniques to develop feature rich applications using wxPython.

Please check **www.PacktPub.com** for information on our titles

CPSIA information can be obtained at www.ICGtesting.com
225947LV00003B/53/P

9 781849 512985